INSPIRE HIS DEVOTION

Activate A Man's Masculine Instinct
To Protect, Provide, And Cherish,
By Learning To Receive Him

Zak Roedde

ISBN: 9798388983473

Printed in the United States of America

CONTENTS

Title Page

Copyright

INTRODUCTION 1

CHAPTER 1 6

CHAPTER 2 23

CHAPTER 3 37

CHAPTER 4 47

CHAPTER 5 59

CHAPTER 6 72

CHAPTER 7 84

CHAPTER 8 102

CHAPTER 9 116

CONCLUSION 132

INTRODUCTION

MEN NEED TO BE RECEIVED

Are you being fully cherished by a strong and powerful man in a committed relationship right now?

Are you receiving kisses, hugs, and amazing sex frequently and passionately?

Are you receiving date nights and special events planned both in and out of the home?

Are you receiving the help you need?

Are you receiving jewelry, food, and spending money?

Are you receiving all the compliments and emotional support that you need?

Are you receiving the competent and loving advice, leadership, and boundaries you need to feel safe to let go?

Are you receiving the strength and power from a man that turns you on with nearly uncontrollable levels of attraction in and out of the bedroom?

Experiencing all of these things isn't some unattainable fantasy, it can and should be every woman's reality. So if the answer is 'no' to any of these questions, ask yourself, 'why?'

You are probably a loving woman with a huge heart, and you probably try so hard to get what you want and need in your love life. You have probably put in plenty of effort to make your dates or relationships work. Yet you continue to be disappointed and get far less in return than you need to thrive.

What is going on here?

Many women who don't get the love they need start to convince themselves that they are not giving enough of themselves to a man.

Or that they are not giving in the right way.

They believe that if only they tried harder, if only they put in more effort, if only they could show a man how much they care, things would be different.

There are endless books and resources out there that try to convince women that the problem is they just aren't loving a man properly.

There are even books and resources out there to help women better understand how a man needs to receive love, so that women can give love more effectively and thus get the love they need in return.

The problem is that this advice is pointing women in the completely wrong direction. Even if it gets a woman some results, it cannot ever get her what she truly needs:

A strong, powerful, and devoted man who cherishes her and always considers her feelings and needs. Every day. Sustainably, long past the honeymoon period, for the rest of her life.

Without her trying to 'do' anything to receive that kind of love.

But contrary to what so many women believe, the only way for you to get that kind of love from a man is to stop trying to 'give' love to a man. Instead, you must focus entirely on receiving what a man gives you. Yes, I understand this may sounds crazy and possibly confusing, but stick with me here:

Any advice that teaches women how to love a man is built on a fallacy. A fallacy so huge, that it has resulted in the needless suffering of hundreds of millions of women (and men, but especially women).

The fallacy is that men need to be given love by a woman to be happy in a relationship, and to be inspired to love her back.

This fallacy is based on a misunderstanding of men, what inspires them, what they need, and how they are instinctually wired.

A man doesn't need to be 'given' love by his woman. He needs to have his love received.

He doesn't need a woman who is thoughtful and considerate, anticipating his needs and desires to make him happy.

Even if he thinks he does, even if he enjoys it on some level.

He needs a woman who is expressive, receptive, and grateful

when receiving anything from him. His touch, time, gifts, money, advice, direction, compliments, support, and everything he does for her.

When a woman is able to receive effectively, she activates a man's masculine instincts to want to give even more.

When she is unable to receive effectively, or when she focuses on giving, she turns off a man's masculine instincts from wanting to give to her, meet her needs, and ensure she feels cherished.

There are deep biological reasons for this, which this book will explain.

Unfortunately, most women have no idea how to turn on a man's instincts, nor do they realize that they are inadvertently doing many things to turn those instincts off. They struggle with receiving a man's gifts, and they struggle to stop giving. The result is that they are not experiencing the kind of relationship they want to have, or they aren't experiencing a relationship at all. This is a direct consequence of not knowing how to receive.

Receiving is not nearly as easy and straightforward as it sounds. If it was, it wouldn't require an entire book to explain it. It requires letting go of all control, and most women are stuck in control patterns when interacting with men. Some of those control patterns are obvious, some are much more subtle. But all of them are preventing a woman from being able to receive and to stop giving, which means a man will be demotivated from wanting to give to her.

I'm going to help you change that. I am going to show you what you are doing, why you are doing it, and how to shift it.

This book will show you exactly how you are not receiving men / a man, and what to do about it.

The information in this book is what I used to...

...teach my wife how to inspire me to cherish her as much as possible.

...teach my single women clients how to attract a man and inspire him to cherish them as much as possible.

... teach my partnered women clients how to inspire their man to cherish them as much as possible.

Whether you are single or in a relationship right now, learning this information will teach you how to do the same thing.

This book isn't just for women either, while I've marketed it and written it as if I am speaking to women, any man can use what I teach here to better lead any woman out of her control patterns so that he will be inspired to cherish her. This information is what I have taught my men clients with incredible results too.

The magic of receiving is the big secret to inspiring a man to give you the world. Now you are about to learn how to do it.

CHAPTER 1

MASCULINE AND FEMININE INSTINCT

If you want a man who gives you love in all the ways you need every day, stop trying to give him love. He doesn't need it (even if he thinks he does), nor is he inspired by it (even if he thinks he is).

I know this statement may sound very counter-intuitive and may even seem to go against your own experiences.

Isn't the golden rule to treat others the way you want to be treated? If you want love, shouldn't you give love?

Further, if you didn't give a man love, wouldn't you become a cold, selfish, and heartless taker? Wouldn't it be cruel to stop giving love to a man when you love him?

If you're asking these types of questions, I get it. I've been there. The perspective I will be sharing with you would have sounded insane to me only a few years ago. I used to believe that healthy relationships were give and take, both man and woman 'giving' and 'receiving'. Trying to both love each other in the unique way that they needed.

That's how my marriage functioned during our first few years together. I'd try to get my wife to give me more touch and give me more compliments because that's how I felt loved. She'd try to get me to spend more time with her and do more nice things with her because that's how she felt loved. The marriage was functional, but I was not as inspired to cherish her as the men in Disney movies and romance books are with their woman. It felt like a lot of work.

I loved my wife, I wanted her to be happy, and I didn't enjoy it when she was unhappy. But it required willpower for me to give her everything she needed. That is not how it should feel for a man to meet every need of his beloved. It should feel effortless and fun, sustainably for an entire lifetime. If it doesn't feel this way for a man, it means something is wrong.

I knew something was wrong in my marriage, but I didn't understand the problem or how to solve it until I learned about instinct. Once you learn about the different but complementary instincts that men and women have, everything you have experienced in your love life starts to make a lot more sense. The solution to transform your love life also becomes crystal clear.

The problem was that my wife and I were not listening to our instincts or relating to each other through our instincts. Once we learned how to do so, everything started changing for the better very quickly. I learned how to feel desire to cherish my wife every day, like when we were first dating. I led her to stop giving, and showed her how to receive everything I gave her in a way that inspired me to give more. My touch. My plans. My compliments. My support. My advice. My help. My leadership.

I began to realize that I didn't need my wife to make me feel loved. In fact, I didn't need to feel loved, period. That was a wound. What I really needed was to feel received. That need to feel and be received only began to get met as I taught my wife how to receive me and everything I gave her.

As this dynamic shifted, our marriage got much better, for both of us. I started to feel increasingly responsible and motivated to take care of my wife and make sure her needs were met. Instead of it feeling like work, it started feeling like fun.

As I made these shifts in my own marriage, I discovered through the success in my clients love-lives that this information can be universally applied. The reason why is because all men have the same masculine instincts as I do, and every woman can learn how to activate those instincts to inspire a man to cherish her.

It's OK if you are somewhat skeptical. I expect you to be. In fact, you should be very skeptical. For now, try your best to suspend your disbelief, and get ready to understand men in a way you never have before... Ready? Here we go.

At the core of every man is his masculine instinct. The instinct to lead a woman, to provide for a woman, to protect a woman, and to cherish a woman. To make her dreams come true by taking care of her emotionally, physically, sexually, financially, and spiritually.

For many men today, this instinct is buried under a lifetime of wounding and unnatural belief systems. This unfortunately means that many men are not being led by those instincts, and may not even be aware of their instincts. But those instincts are there, in every single man. Waiting to be activated, by a woman like you.

I'm going to tell you exactly how to activate those instincts in a man, but before I do, we must talk about why a man has those instincts in the first place. To do so, I'm going to give you simplified lesson of cavemen thousands of years ago. Don't take this lesson too literally or you aren't going to have any fun or learn the underlying message I am trying to convey. This is to give you a very basic understanding of how and why men and women are programmed the way they are, and maybe give you a few laughs in the process. It doesn't matter if you are an evolutionist, or believe God put us here 6000 years ago, or believe we were made by aliens in test-tubes, or anything in-between.

Regardless of how we initially got here, it's our instincts that have kept our genes replicating for thousands of years, and that's what this lesson is about. So close your eyes for a moment and picture a cave-man. Make him extra cute in your imagination. Put him in a top hat and overalls with big yellow buttons just for the hell of it. Got it? OK.

Now, let's give him a super creative name. Let's call him 'Fred.'

Fred is your great great great great (etc x1000) granddaddy.

How is it that Fred is alive without going to school to learn how to be a caveman and without the advanced language we have today?

Because of instinct. Fred's instincts lead him to do certain behaviors so he stays alive, and to ensure his genes replicate. His instincts do this by making him feel certain emotions which compel him into certain behaviors which improve the chances of genetic survival.

Fred's instincts are programmed to make him feel hunger when he needs calories. His hunger will compel him to seek out food and eat it.

Fred's instincts are programmed to make him feel fear when he is in danger to avoid the threat. His fear will compel him to be cautious and stay in his territory near his cave and tribe.

Fred's instincts are also programmed to make him feel anger when being attacked. His anger will compel him to aggressively fight off an attacker.

All of these feelings maximize the chances that Fred will stay alive long enough to replicate his genes through sex, so that his offspring can do the exact same thing, repeated generation after generation.

To replicate his genes, Fred's instincts are programmed to make him feel horny when he sees a cave-lady (let's call her Wilma) walking by him in a lovely summer dress. His horniness will compel him to court her on a few dates in cave-people town and eventually take her back to his own cave to show her his cave-art collection.

By the way, Wilma is your great great great great (etc x1000) grandmama.

Fred wants to mate for life by the way, he isn't doing any one night-stand. He isn't 'that cave-guy'. He is claiming her as his woman and putting a ring on that.

Once mated, Fred finds himself with new emotions that are driving his behaviors to take care of Wilma, because of his instincts. While both cave-men and cave-ladies have similar survival instincts, this part of his instincts that I will be describing is exclusive to cave-men. This is his 'masculine' instincts.

His masculine instincts will create a feeling of strong desire to provide for and protect Wilma. That desire will compel him to go out and find more rocks for his cave furniture, so Wilma feels more comfortable. It will compel him to find more woolly mammoth meat, so Wilma is fed. It will compel him to protect Wilma, even risking his own life from sabre-toothed tigers to keep her safe. He will feel a form of primitive satisfaction and joy when doing this primitive form of 'cherishing' his mate.

The question is, why would his masculine instincts compel him to cherish Wilma. What's in it for him? Why doesn't he just relax after impregnating her and play cave-man videogames all day?

His masculine instincts are compelling him to do these things to keep his genes alive. The better a job Fred does with providing for and protecting Wilma, the higher the chance that Wilma has healthy well-nourished cave-children which grow up to survive, thrive, and reproduce. Those cave-children will have his genes in them. His genes have been programmed to do everything possible for optimal chances of that successful replication.

"But why can't the cave-man take care of the children?"

This answer should be obvious to everyone, but sadly today it isn't. Men have bodies better designed than women to hunt, build, and protect. Men's bodies are also incapable of growing a child or nursing a child. Whereas women's bodies are perfectly suited for growing a child and nursing a child.

The instinctual programming of men and women complements our physical differences. Modern day society and technology gives men and women more flexibility with gender-roles, but our instincts were programmed for when we did not have such flexibility.

If Fred didn't have masculine instincts to provide and protect Wilma, he would get lazy and play cave-man videogames all day.

His children would grow up malnourished and developmentally stunted, or possibly die because Wilma didn't get the provision and protection that she needed to give the children optimal nourishment and nurturing. The result is that Fred's genes would probably die out and be replaced by the genes of other cave-men that have instinctual programming better suited for genetic survival. Which means you would never have been born.

While this may be the deeper reason for Fred cherishing his cave-wife, he isn't acting on that cognitively. He isn't thinking *"I need to do all this stuff for my wife so I can have healthy kids who continue to pass on my genes."*

That would really kill the romance, wouldn't it?

Instead, it's much simpler. Fred simply feels love and responsibility for Wilma, and that love and sense of responsibility compels him into a feeling of strong desire to provide for and protect her. It doesn't feel like work to do this. His actions feel effortless and purposeful, and dare I say it; fun. There is a word I use to describe this emotional state of effortless action-based love a man has for his woman:

'Devotion.'

To Fred, his Devotion feels like it's for his wife because it's directed at her. But on a deeper, much less romantic level, his Devotion is simply for his genes and their survival.

I'll pause my cave-people story for a moment to interject something about love: I love my wife, I am devoted to my wife. When I look at her, I feel inspired to make her the happiest woman in the world, and that love is real and beautiful. Just because that love is due to my genes basically manipulating my behaviors to ensure their survival, doesn't make it any less real or beautiful. It's important to understand how genes come into play here, but don't let it squash the beauty that is a man's love for his woman.

OK, back to the cave-people.

Fred's Devotion compels him into naturally taking on what I call the 'giving' role. He is giving his provision and protection to Wilma through his own initiative, out of love.

Wilma is in what I call the 'receiving' role. She is receiving his provision and protection without her needing to lead him to do it, or nag him to do it, or hint at him doing it, or manipulate him into doing it.

Fred feels good being in the giver role, because that is maximizing his chance of gene survival. His genes are programmed to make him feel good for doing what he should to ensure his genes survive. For cherishing his cave-wife. He is programmed to need to give, to feel as happy as possible. Why does he feel happy when he's doing his job? Because his genes are programmed to give him that emotional reward for doing his job to maximize their chance of survival and replication. If he didn't get that hit of happiness, he wouldn't be motivated to hunt that mammoth and bring it back to Wilma so his genes survive, and then his genes would die out.

Wilma feels good being in the receiver role, because that is maximizing her chance of gene survival. Her genes are also programmed to make her feel good when receiving her cave-husband's help. For being cherished by him. She is programmed to need to receive, to feel as happy as possible. Why does she feel happy when she's receiving gifts? Because her genes are programmed to give her that reward for doing what will maximize their chance of survival and replication. If she didn't get that hit of happiness, she wouldn't be motivated to relax and allow Fred to provide for and protect her so her genes survive, and then her genes would die out.

Fred feels good being in the giving role because of his masculine instincts. Wilma feels good being in the receiver role because of her feminine instincts. Both masculine and feminine instincts know that their genes have the best chance of survival if the woman is given the resources and protection to relax and have a successful pregnancy, birthing, and raising of the offspring. Offspring which contains both of their genes.

That is why Fred feels the need to provide and protect, and have those gifts received.

That is why Wilma feels the need to receive provision and protection.

Now let's apply this to modern day human beings. After all, the majority of my readers were born in the last century, and only a small minority of my readers are cave-people who have been unfrozen recently after thousands of years stuck in ice, so we've got to make this applicable.

Humans today are programmed with the exact same instincts as cave-people. Nothing has changed. Our environment has changed. The way society is structured has changed. The complexity of having a relationship and family in modern day society has changed. The amount of social conditioning and complexity of our belief systems have changed. But under it all, we've got those same exact basic instincts as cave-people. In fact, most mammalian species do (as do many other non-mammal species). It's survival of the fittest. Not just the fittest bodies, but the fittest instinctual programming, and men being programmed to give and women being programmed to receive is simply smart programming.

Just like cavemen, modern-men have an instinct to give provision, protection, and cherishing. This instinct has created our core need to 'be received'.

Just like cave-ladies, modern-women have an instinct to receive provision, protection, and cherishing. This instinct has created a woman's core need to 'be cherished'.

When a man is in the giving role cherishing his woman, he is in his 'masculine' energy. It's a penetrative, strong, and loving energy leading towards the outcome he wants to give her. He gives to her not out of obligation, or to control her, or take from her, but simply to put a smile on her face and make her life better.

When a woman is in the receiving role receiving that cherishing, she is in her 'feminine' energy. It's an energy of opening up to, flowing with, allowing, and letting go of control to receive the outcome she is being given. She receives without trying to get her man to do anything.

Being in these energies is natural and based on our instinctual programming. When we conform with this programming and stay in our natural energy, there is natural 'polarity'.

When I speak of polarity, think of magnets with two 'poles'. A north pole and a south pole.

What happens when you stick two north or two south poles together? They repel each other.

But what happens when you stick a north pole with a south pole together? Instant attraction and connection. They come together as one.

Our energies work in the same way. When the man is in his masculine energy in the giving role, and the woman is in her feminine energy in the receiving role, there is instant attraction and connection. They come together as one. If both man and woman know how to stay in their natural roles, they stay attracted and connected to each other their whole lives. That is polarity.

Polarity can only be created with masculine 'giving' energy and feminine 'receiving' energy. These energetic roles are the foundation of all 'gender roles' we see in our society. When you look around at many of our traditional norms (which are currently being eroded) you see how these instinctual roles of giving and receiving have been ingrained in our culture far beyond the cave-people basics of giving and receiving resources and protection.

In dances, the man physically gives his leadership, the woman receives it.

On dates, the man gives the time and place and leads or drives the woman to it, she receives this leadership.

With chivalry, men give their direction by pulling out chairs and opening doors. They also give protection by walking on the outside of the sidewalk closest to cars.

It's typically men who do the present buying and the compliment giving, to make women feel special.

When proposing, the man gives the ring (and his offer of lifetime commitment), the woman chooses to receive it (or not).

When married, the man used to be the sole provider who would go out and work to provide food and shelter, the woman would receive it and take care of the home and children.

On a larger scale, it's the men that go to war, to protect all women and all offspring, the women receive that protection.

Did these gender roles arise because of (now outdated) social conditioning?

No. These gender roles arose because of our instincts. Our instincts have not changed one bit in the last century or in the last several thousand years, though for many of us they have become buried and suppressed.

It was instinct that created these roles and embedded them into our cultural framework for thousands of years, inside and outside of relationships. Whereas it is more recent social conditioning that is eroding and blurring the gender lines of giving and receiving by covering up our natural instinctual drives. Even going so far as to judge those instincts as 'wrong' or 'toxic' or 'wounding'.

These social changes are often celebrated by many today as 'progress', but it is nothing to celebrate. Men are meant to be in the giving role, and women are meant to be in the receiving role. All the time. When these gender roles blur or invert, men become increasingly unhappy. Their masculine instincts start to shut off and they stop feeling Devotion for women. When men stop feeling Devotion for women, they stop cherishing women. When men stop cherishing women, women's needs go unmet and they become increasingly unhappy too.

If a woman wants to be cherished by a man and made to feel like the most special woman on earth, she needs to learn how to inspire a man into his rightful place in the giving role. To inspire a man into the giving role, she needs to get very good at being in the receiving role.

She needs to learn how to activate his masculine instinct to give. Not out of obligation. Not to get something back in return. But simply out of love. Out of Devotion.

To be clear, I am not proposing women need to go back to the 1950's and spend all day cleaning diapers and sinks if they want to be cherished. There were many lonely, unhappy housewives who were not being cherished back then. There were many women who were seen as 'less than' a man and treated like servants rather than cherished as women. In the 1950's, and throughout much of human history, many of the gender roles performed by men and women were more of act. It was done largely out of necessity rather than out of self worth and true embodiment of our masculine and feminine energies.

There were many great things with how men and women operated differently in the 1950's which makes sense to shift back to. However, what I propose in this book is something the world has never seen before on a large scale in any culture throughout recorded human history. It is far more revolutionary and far more fulfilling for women (and men) than the 1950's ever were.

Instead of taking men and women back to the 1950's, I'm taking you forward in time to the 2050's. You just get to start a few decades early before the masses are ready for it. They are not ready to let go of the woundings and social conditioning that is keeping them stuck. But if you have gotten this far in this book and it's resonating, you are in the special minority. You might just be ready.

When I first began to understand how a man and woman's instincts worked, my marriage was experiencing a lot of problems. We were having many fights and we were feeling increasingly less connected and attracted to each other. We tried so hard to make it work to stop fighting and rekindle the huge amount of attraction and connection we had during our first year together. But every time we thought we fixed the problem, the solution didn't last.

Nothing worked, until I began to listen to my masculine instincts, and led my marriage based on my instincts. My goal was to feel as much Devotion for my wife as possible. By learning how to do this, I turned a slightly better than mediocre marriage into an amazing marriage that gets more incredible by the day.

One of the most important changes: I taught my wife how to let go of control and receive my love.

What I am referring to when I say 'receive my love' is being receptive and grateful to all of the ways I loved her.

Giving her hugs, kisses, and all forms of touch.

Giving her gifts, meals, and spending money.

Giving time to be with her and making plans to spend time with her.

Giving her compliments, advice, direction, and support.

Giving her help and assistance to make her life easier.

Giving her expectations of who does what in the household, and what is and isn't acceptable.

Giving her feedback and direction on how she communicates and interacts with me.

The first few examples are typically easier for most women to receive. The last few may be more challenging.

But all of these are gifts. All are given with effortless Devotion, only because my wife now knows how to receive those gifts.

The more that I taught my wife how to receive my gifts, the more motivated I became to give them. The more gifts that I gave her, the more cherished she felt.

Interestingly, the more cherished she felt, the less I wanted to receive gifts from her. Her gratitude, respect, joy and reception of my gifts was all I needed. It's all any man needs, as you'll soon find out.

I had no idea a relationship or marriage could be this amazing, natural, and effortless. I had no idea that by operating on instincts and shifting into our natural gender roles of giving and receiving, it was possible to create a sustainable never-ending honeymoon.

A sustainable never-ending honeymoon is real when you know how to create it.

The better my wife has become at receiving my gifts, the more I enjoyed giving her those gifts. Which motivated me to be increasingly competent, centered, and generous. The more I became competent, centered, and generous, the more my wife wanted to receive from me and the more she enjoyed receiving from me. This is all instinctual.

See how that works? It creates a perfect energy loop where we both become energized and fulfilled by being in our respective roles.

As long as both partners stay in these roles, this energy continues to build, and the honeymoon period is never ending. When partners don't know how to stay in these roles, our needs go unmet, we start to feel increasingly bad, and the relationship becomes increasingly less enjoyable and more filled with problems.

What I discovered and implemented in my marriage was so ground-breaking and life-changing that I wrote multiple books about it and created an entire coaching program called 'Relationship Of Your Dreams Academy'.

In the Academy I have a team of coaches who have transformed their own love lives by implementing what is taught in this book.

My team of coaches and I helped hundreds of my women clients in the Academy by showing them how to shift their communication and behaviors to inspire a man into devotion.

We also have helped our men clients learn to lovingly and competently lead a woman into making these shifts so she can be fully receptive and inspiring in a relationship.

This work is universally applicable, and not an unattainable fantasy. Anyone can do it with enough understanding, courage, self awareness, and persistence.

This book is going to show you exactly what that looks like, and how to make it happen.

You're going to learn how to create what I call 'the relationship of your dreams'.

CHAPTER 2

WOUNDING

We live in a world today where most men are not living from their instincts. They are not in the giving role, or they go back and forth between the giving and receiving role. You can recognize such men based on certain behaviors. Here are a few possible ones that men may exhibit, it is far from an exhaustive list:

They lead a woman to pay for dates, or let a woman pay for dates if she volunteers.

They split bills with a woman and may expect her to work to financially contribute to the household.

They want the woman to initiate and make plans, or they don't stop her if she tries.

They look for advice, support, and compliments from a woman.

They want a woman to initiate physical touch and sex.

They want a woman to anticipate their needs, just like their mother.

They want a woman to buy them gifts, at minimum for birthdays, Christmas, and Valentines day.

Or, they do much or all of the 'giving', initiating, planning, buying, etc, but it done out of obligation rather than Devotion.

All of this is due to wounding. Wounding which covers up a man's natural instincts to Devote to a woman by being in the giving role all of the time, and only desiring his woman to receive.

When I speak of wounding, I am referring to the childhood trauma received as a boy. When a boy experiences any kind of trauma (which could be as small as his parents judging him) he begins to suppress part of himself unconsciously. If his suppression is substantial enough, he will get stuck in a state of arrested development, and never grow into manhood where he feels compelled to be in the giving role all the time.

For example, if a boy is raised by a single mother, he will almost certainly not be given the opportunity to grow through all vital stages of emotional development into manhood, because he didn't have a father figure to guide him. Nor did he have a feminine mother to take care of as he grew up, because she stayed firmly in the giving (masculine) role. Single moms reading this, don't panic, you can avoid much of this by shifting yourself starting now.

Wounding can happen due to parents divorcing, parents in reverse gender roles, parents who switch gender roles, parents who didn't allow a child's full emotional expression, parents who were neglectful or overbearing, parents who are emotionally or sexually abusive, and much more. But it doesn't need to be extreme examples like this, it can also be much more subtle. Wounding can happen even in happy households with two loving parents.

The end result is always the same however: The man doesn't feel compelled to be in the giving role to lead and cherish, and so the woman he chooses doesn't get the cherishing she needs.

The first couple years of my marriage perfectly illustrate this phenomenon.

When I met my wife, I truly thought I must be the most developed and healthy man on planet earth. Comical looking back, but I did have a lot going for me. I was supremely confident in myself, I loved myself unconditionally, I had cultivated a great sense of humor, amazing social skills, leadership skills, and had a proven successful track record with meeting and dating women.

But I had some major glaring character flaws too, specifically with my disinterest of being in the giving role:

I told my wife to pay for our second date to 'keep it even'.

I made her travel an hour to see me, and didn't even pay for her subway fare.

I had her do a lot of the planning for things we were going to do.

I even had her pay for her own meal on her birthday because I didn't like spending money on anyone (including myself) unless it was an investment.

OK that last one is truly embarrassing to admit, even after seven years.

All of my issues boil down to my masculine instincts to Devote from the giving role being suppressed. I was a good leader in many ways, but it wasn't coming from a place of feeling that deep desire and sense of responsibility to give. To be in the role as provider and protector for my woman.

When I use the term 'role' in reference to a man, think of it like a job with great responsibility. Like a teacher. If you were to send your child to school, you'd expect the teacher to want to be in the teacher role, right? If the teacher wanted to play around with the other children and make paper airplanes all day, you would consider that an abdication of his (or her) duty, yes? Any sane person would agree that the teacher should be in the teacher role, and should want to be there, because that's his (or her) responsibility.

The same is true for the giving role. That is where the man is supposed to be with his woman. That's his role, his responsibility. When he is healed, he will want to be there and he will be very competent at being there. It won't ever feel like an obligation, it will feel like a joy. He will not enjoy his time with a woman if he isn't there.

That was what I was missing when I first met my wife. I could be in the giving role energetically and I often was there (in non-financial ways), but I didn't feel responsible for being there. I was like the teacher who was competent enough to be in the teaching role when he felt like it, but often made paper airplanes and made fart jokes instead.

What I didn't know at the time was that despite all of the healing and self development I had done, I had a deep wound that kept me very stingy. This showed up when giving anything, but especially giving anything with a financial price-tag. The wound was built upon a fear that if I gave too much, I wouldn't have enough left for myself and then my needs would be unmet. I couldn't consciously feel that fear, but that fear dictated many of my behaviors.

This fear wasn't logical. I was debt free, had more money in savings and investments than 90% of the population, and I was perfectly capable of making more. But logic doesn't matter with childhood wounding.

I had wonderful loving parents growing up, but I was put in daycare early so my parents could continue medical school. Some boys and girls can do a (relatively) good job of adapting to this unnatural early separation. But I did not adapt well. While I have no real memory of this, I still to this day can feel myself as that little baby boy, with a sense of fear and abandonment, emotional needs unmet when I just needed my mommy to comfort me. There is much sadness that comes up when I feel into that, as there would be for most men and women, if they are in touch with their unmet childhood needs.

My unconscious coping mechanism that I carried for most of my life (which stemmed from that wound) was to be very conservative in everything I gave, so I always had enough left for myself. The wound was severe enough that I didn't feel a desire to take care of anyone and their needs, other than myself and my own needs. I did not feel responsible for anyone other than myself.

Like so many grown men today, I was trapped in boyhood. But unlike many grown men today, I had broken free of any social or cultural obligations to pretend to be responsible in the giving role. The sad truth today is that many men will still go through the motions of paying for dates and doing all of the things they are 'supposed' to do for a woman. But it's not coming from Devotion, it's coming from being programmed to believe that they are supposed to because they are the man. Or they do it because they think it will get them what they want (ie sex). This is not Devotion, it's cultural servitude.

This isn't a recent phenomenon. It was an issue in the 1950's and long before. Many men acting the part of being men out of obligation and social conditioning, rather than truly feeling that Devotion to be in the giving role from their heart. Boyhood isn't about what you do, it's about why you do it. Boys live for their own pleasure and will have many strategies to get what they want. Many strategies will be obligatory, but it's a means to an end. If they give, it's often to get. But men live to serve their woman (and the world). They give to give. They feel responsible for giving, and they love to have that responsibility. They need to have that responsibility.

For me, I didn't give to get. I gave when I wanted because I enjoyed giving, and I didn't give when I didn't feel like it. When I gave, I gave without a sense of responsibility in my giving. You might be wondering why a woman would ever stay with a man who very clearly demonstrated he wasn't interested in taking the provider role. Especially a woman like my wife, who had more self-worth than most women I had met (which was the main reason I chose her).

She stuck with me because despite my shortcomings, I had the confidence, charm, and self-worth to make her fall for me. Without that, she would have gotten too turned off by all of the red flags I was showing her, and left.

But the more relevant reason she stuck with me is because despite having high self-worth, she also had her own wounding, which was very complementary to mine. She was hyper-independent. I do not know what caused this in her childhood, because she also had relatively healthy loving parents. But something did. That wounding covered up her feminine instinct to be provided for and cherished. Her instincts weren't completely buried. She certainly made it very clear that she wasn't happy about me not paying for her birthday dinner. But a lot of things I did either didn't bother her, or bothered her much less than they would have, had her feminine instinct been fully online.

If her feminine instincts were fully online, staying with me the way I was would have been intolerably painful.

There are many woundings that women can have which will blunt or fully suppress the emotional warnings given from feminine instincts. I'm going to focus on the three biggest below, and it's possible for a woman to have more than one:

1. The independence wound – This is the main wound that my wife had. The wound was based on the belief that her worth comes from how capable she is, and she was very capable. This meant that she would often have resistance to me doing things for her, because 'she can do it herself.' Some women can have this wound but have very low self-worth. They are hyper-independent because they have a deep belief that they are not worthy of being taken care of. But whether high self worth or low self worth, this wound causes women to lack trust in men as she believes that she is better off taking care of herself. This tends to attract men like me who are also hyper-independent and not interested being in the giving role. These men aren't necessarily takers, but they aren't givers either.

2. The giver wound – This wound is based on a woman's belief that her worth comes from what she can do or give to a man. At the extreme, women with this wound tend to stay in the giving role, and spend their money on a man, nurture him, give him advice, and support him. She becomes the care-taker instead of her being taken care of. This tends to attract men who are unconsciously

looking for a mother. These men are receivers or takers.

3. The doormat wound – This wound is based on a woman's belief that she has little worth and doesn't deserve provision. At the extreme, women with this wound will accept breadcrumbs of provision, yet will do whatever a man tells her to do. She will do what he wants to meet his needs even if her needs aren't being met. This tends to attract controlling men who want to subjugate (rather than devotionally lead) a woman, while giving little in return. These men are takers.

A woman's wounds will result in her attracting men who won't provide for her the way that she needs because of his own wounds. But worse, the woman's wounds, if not addressed, will also result in her perpetuating the man's wounding, rather than activating his masculine instincts to step into the giving role and Devote to her.

In my marriage, my wife wasn't the one to activate my masculine instincts. My son Mikah did.

Mikah was our first child, and his birth was a nightmare for my wife and me. He was born by emergency C-section, at only 4 pounds, almost dead from starvation. He had multiple seizures during his first hour of life, and he was emergency evacuated to another hospital hours after being born before either of us could hold him.

But it got worse; not only did he get significant brain damage from the seizures and near-starvation, he also had an extremely rare genetic condition that would mean his development would be significantly stunted, if he survived.

Just to rub some lemon juice in the wounds, he was hooked up to a ventilator and IV for the first two weeks of his life and not breastfed or bottle fed, to supposedly combat serious blood sugar issues. It was very clear (to me) that his blood sugar issues were because he was born starved, and then continued to be underfed by IV and almost nothing by bottle. It didn't take a rocket scientist to figure that out, but apparently a team of doctors couldn't. While I was busy fighting doctors to feed him more against their normal very rigid 'procedures', they were fighting with me to grant permission to put him on drugs to nuke his thyroid to 'fix' his blood sugar. Completely insane and archaic.

But his life and death situation was a blessing in disguise. It put me in a state of emotional agony beyond anything I had ever experienced. I had never loved anyone like I loved Mikah. I had no idea it was possible to love someone that much, he made me question what love even was. From the moment he was born, all of my priorities in life shifted. All I cared about was that he was given every opportunity to develop as normally as he could, at whatever cost to myself that was necessary. I needed him to be safe and happy.

Yet he was neither safe nor happy. Instead, he was drugged practically into a coma on anti-seizure meds with very serious long term side effects, he was being underfed without gaining weight, and he was getting far less touch and love than necessary for optimal development. He needed me to get him some damn calories so he could be taken off the machines and eventually taken home. I felt 100% responsible for making sure that happened as quickly as possible. If not me, then who?

That situation is what activated my masculine instincts to provide and protect. Had he been a healthy child and we took him home right away, I do not know if my instincts would have come fully online. But because he was trapped in a hospital with incompetent and dangerous care, my instincts were screaming at me to take charge and do something. That requires masculine energy. A woman could also be activated into that role if she had no man to take that burden from her. But men are the ones who are naturally supposed to be there. When their instincts are online.

Thankfully, my instincts had come online.

I took charge of everything. I shifted for the first time in my life into being fully in the giving role and gave Mikah my full protection and provision. I did absolutely everything I could to allow my wife as much bonding time with him as possible and to stop the dangerous and unnecessary drug and procedure interventions. After two weeks, we got him off the machines, and after three weeks we got him home.

Everything I gave him was inspired by love. By Devotion. It was always natural to give, it was completely effortless. I couldn't have done anything else without causing myself pain from abdicating my responsibility. I experienced that Devotion right up until his death, at our home, at six months of age. There was nothing we could have done, it was his genetic condition and it was inevitable (in hindsight). A tragically short life, but one where he was given so much loving care.

What he taught me though, has created a movement, and is changing the world.

Being in the giving role with Mikah wasn't 'fun' due to the circumstances. It isn't always fun. But there was always a 'rightness' to it. It felt like 'my role'. That was the first taste I had of being in the giving role because of Devotion; giving provision, protection, and cherishing purely for the sake of giving. There was no going back. My instincts had been activated fully, and ever after, I became obsessed with my mission of trying to feel that level of Devotion with my wife.

Mikah activated the frequency of Devotion in me, but that didn't mean I felt the same way with my wife off the bat. I wanted to, yet she did so many things to make that impossible. It only became possible to stay in the frequency of Devotion with my wife by teaching her the frequency of Reception. By teaching her how to receive me as her man.

For a woman to be in this frequency, she must fully respect her man as her leader, protector, and provider. She must not try to energetically give to him or lead him. She must be fully open to all of his gifts and feel her need for his gifts. She must receive all of those gifts with (genuine) gratitude. That is what a man needs from his woman.

Before my instincts became activated, I could be reasonably happy in my marriage without that need being met, because it was suppressed. But after my instincts became activated, I needed to be in the giving role with my wife, always. I needed to feel that same level of Devotion to her that I felt for Mikah.

A man being in this role isn't a want. Or a desire. Or a preference. He is programmed for it. He cannot thrive and be at his best without being in this role and without being received consistently by his woman. He needs to give his touch, his time, his money, his service, his support, his love, his leadership, and his boundaries, and he needs all of that to be received by his woman.

The more his instinct is online, the more irritation and distress he will feel if he is not in that role with his woman or if his woman doesn't receive him when he tries to be in that role. His instincts will warn him that there is a problem, and that his genes are at risk if he doesn't rectify the problem. It can even cause him emotional pain for his woman to not see him and respect him as 'the giver', 'the provider', 'the protector', and 'the leader' in the relationship. If he doesn't get what he needs from his woman for a long enough period, he may eventually give up trying.

If a man's instincts are very much online, a woman can inspire change in a relationship or during dating extremely quickly by making the shifts outlined in this book. Everything will shift naturally and easily because the man is fully ready to be in that role as soon as a woman learns how to receive him in that role.

But if a man is deeply wounded, he may be out of touch with this need, or he may not feel it as a need, because his instinct is suppressed. Or his instinct may be online, but it causes him to be highly emotionally reactive and even abusive when he is not being respected and received. If a woman is in a relationship with or dating such a man, these shifts will be much slower and much more painful.

But they will still be possible.

Progress will also be much slower if a woman tries making these shifts when her feminine instinct is deeply suppressed. To make these shifts, your instinct must be felt. The more it's felt, the faster the shifts occur. The less it's felt, the slower the shifts occur. Teaching you to be in the receiving role when your instincts are deeply suppressed underneath a lifetime of wounding would be like teaching you to have sex if you didn't feel horny or pleasure. Sure you could go through the motions of sex with various techniques and positions, but it's unnatural until you feel the signals your body is giving you.

This book is simply pointing you back to the truth of your instincts. Unlike most dating and relationship advice which is conceptual and 'heady', my intention is to help put words to the truth that your body already knows, once you learn how to listen to it. I am not here to guide you. Your body is here to guide you, and I am here to show you how and why to listen to it and trust it.

To a man or woman whose instincts are already fully online, what I teach is as natural as if I was telling you to make spaghetti and put it in your mouth when you are hungry, instead of up your butt. If I told you it's natural to put spaghetti up your butt 'some of the time', you'd think there was something seriously wrong with me. Your instincts would know the truth that putting spaghetti up your butt doesn't serve you, and that the only natural thing to do with spaghetti is to eat it with your mouth.

That is why what I teach can be hard for many men and women to resonate with if their instincts are deeply suppressed. It can seem extreme, rigid, restricting, regressive, and old-fashioned.

"Why can't the woman sometimes give to the man and why can't the man sometimes receive from the woman?"

To me, this question is the same as asking why you can't sometimes put spaghetti up your butt.

Because when instincts are fully activated, the woman won't want to sometimes give. The man won't want to sometimes receive... Just like neither man or woman will want to sometimes put spaghetti up their butt. They could do these things, they just won't want to.

A woman's wounds might make her want to sometimes give. A

man's wounds might make him want to sometimes receive. But catering to wounding will never result in healing, and it will never result in the natural polarity, attraction, and ease that can only be experienced by operating from instincts.

If your instincts are offline or significantly suppressed, this book will be more challenging to get through and take in. But if you are in this situation, don't give up. Continue reading it with an open mind and try to see how it could be right. The more you expose yourself to this information and try to understand it, the more it will activate your instincts. On that note, be sure to read my other books too.

I transformed my marriage by learning how to trust and follow my instincts. I've also transformed the love-lives of hundreds of my clients by teaching them how to trust their own instincts. What I teach works, and it works universally. Because every man has masculine instincts to give, and every woman has feminine instincts to receive. There are no exceptions, there are only woundings that make it look like there are exceptions.

CHAPTER 3

WHEN A WOMAN'S INSTINCTS ARE ONLINE

If a man's instinct to be in the giving role is not online, any woman he dates or gets into a relationship with will be in for an unpleasant experience. If not immediately, then certainly long term once she's stuck married to him with children.

If her feminine instincts are suppressed, like my wife's were, the experience may be much more tolerable, because she is not fully in touch with her needs. Which means it won't be as painful when those needs go unmet.

But if a woman's feminine instincts are fully online and she is fully in touch with her needs, her emotional experience can be devastatingly painful when those needs don't get met. Enough to make a woman go crazy. Or at least, act crazy.

However, even if a woman's instincts are suppressed, life with a man who isn't in the giving role will never be amazing long-term. Life will also eventually have a way of showing her what a mess she is in. For my wife, that happened after we took our son home from the hospital. Once he was home, she suddenly, for the first time, needed a massive amount of support, leadership, and love from me in a way she never had before.

But even though my instincts were finally activated, I had no idea how to competently be in that role with her. I knew how to be in that role with my son, because I knew how to protect him from doctors and make sure we were pumping breast milk on schedule. But supporting my wife with a newborn at home was a completely different ballgame I felt unqualified for.

I wasn't able to meet her needs by competently being in the giving role with her, and the result was that she became increasingly hostile. She had her bad days before our son was born, but this was different. She became increasingly judgmental, controlling, and angry. She started nagging and blaming and making me question why I even married her. I found myself in a situation I thought I'd never end up in. A situation that I thought only weak men with no backbone would ever end up in. Things had started out so good in our relationship, but it was becoming a blazing dumpster fire. My son was the match that lit it.

To understand why, I will take you back to Fred and Wilma.

Let's say after the wedding, Wilma gets pregnant. If Fred's instincts were online, he would be spending much of his time ensuring that she is safe, well-fed, and comfortable throughout the pregnancy and afterwards.

But what if, hypothetically, his instincts were not online or he didn't know how to do his job to provide and protect?

What would happen is Wilma would not be provided for and protected. She would have to go out of her comfortable cave and forage for food. Not only risking her life, but also expending valuable energy that should be used on the pregnancy. Her sympathetic nervous system becomes activated, which will keep her in a higher state of stress when she needs to relax. This gets harder and harder as she gets bigger and bigger, and almost impossible when her baby is born because she needs to nurse and nurture the baby. Don't even get me started on how much more challenging it becomes when there are multiple children. The added stress will result in smaller babies, with a smaller available milk supply to grow from. If the babies survive, they will likely be stunted in their growth, and be challenged in finding a suitable mate when they grow up. Unlike modern times, less than optimal development often would mean death and the end of that genetic line.

A cave-lady puts herself in an incredibly vulnerable position when she gets pregnant. She must increasingly rely on her male partner to take care of her, because she can't optimally take care of herself or her babies without his help. Being stuck in such a situation where her man can't or won't help is potentially a genetic death sentence, which is why cave-ladies have an instinct to protect themselves from this possibility. If they sense that a caveman is not willing or capable of providing, they will not sexually submit to him.

Modern women have this same instinct. If a woman senses that a man she likes or loves is not willing or capable of being in the giving role, she will be warned primarily with the emotion 'fear'.

Her fear is telling her "WARNING, WARNING, YOUR GENES MAY DIE OUT."

That emotional warning will happen when a man doesn't provide after she has been sexually intimate with him, or after she gets pregnant. But it will also happen before. It will be there warning her to not have sex with him in the first place, to avoid getting trapped in that dynamic where she is pregnant, and he is not providing.

Unfortunately, if a woman's feminine instinct is suppressed, those warnings will be stifled, like trying to hear someone screaming under water. You know you hear something, but what is it? What does it mean? That was what my wife was experiencing with me, until our son was born. After he was born, her instincts also started to wake up, because now she needed me. When she realized she was with a man who seemed incompetent at being able to give her what she needed, she started to feel anxious. That anxiety compelled her into behaviors that only demotivated me from wanting to be in the giving role, even though my instincts to give were fully online.

Have you ever felt anxious with a man? A stupid question I know, of course you have. Every woman has.

But how much time did you spend trying to understand why you felt anxious?

Did you chalk it up to your own wounding and insecurity issues?

Or did you ever think that maybe there is absolutely nothing wrong with you, and your instincts were trying to warn you that something is wrong?

While a woman certainly will have her own share of woundings which can contribute to anxiety, much of it is often coming from her instincts. A woman's instincts are hyper-sensitive to the possibility of not being provided for and protected by a man if she were to submit to him sexually or after she submits to him sexually, because the risk to her genes are enormous.

Her instincts are warning her about the potential of abandonment. At its worst, abandonment occurs when a man completely ditches her through breakup. This would leave her to fend for herself, as he goes off to be with other women. But abandonment can also mean a man who abandons his duties to provide because he isn't there physically or emotionally to take care of his woman. That was what my wife was experiencing.

There are a million things that can set off this instinct in a woman. Things that to a man, are no big deal, and he may perceive her to be 'over-reacting' or 'acting crazy'. But to a woman, it feels very real, because her instincts are flooding her with emotions that are overwhelming.

For example, to many men, looking at other women's butts while with his woman seems harmless. Perhaps inconsiderate, but not something to get worked up over. But a woman will often get reactive and angry, and underneath that reactivity and anger, there is fear. Fear of abandonment.

That's not a wound. Some of that fear and reactivity might be stemming from a wound. But even if the woman was the most healed woman in the world, it would be normal for her to feel at least some discomfort or anxiety. If she doesn't, that suggests a wound stifling her feminine instinct.

If a man has claimed his woman in his heart, she may not get very reactive if he does something like look at another woman, but she will never feel great about it if her instincts are online. However, if he hasn't fully claimed his woman, there will be other small or big red-flags from his behavior and energy. His woman will already be feeling some mild unease about the relationship, and then 'small' things like checking out another woman can set her off.

Other examples that can trigger a woman's instinct include;

A man who complains, because it communicates that he isn't a problem solver and thus can't provide.

A man who wants to go 50/50 on dates, because it communicates that he isn't interested in being her provider.

A man who needs reassurance or compliments to feel good, because it communicates that he needs to be given to, to be able to provide.

A man who waits around for a woman to initiate, because it communicates that he doesn't have the confidence necessary to provide, or that he doesn't like being with her enough to provide.

A man who breaks his word, because it communicates that even if he makes promises that he will provide, he may end up not providing.

A man who tries to lead a woman to sex before commitment, because it communicates that he may have no interest in providing.

A man who was giving a certain amount of time, affection, compliments, and energy to a woman, but it decreases over time or suddenly, without him telling her why. Because it communicates that his provision may only be temporary.

If a woman is very in touch with her feminine instinct, she will feel a lot of feelings when a man communicates in any way that he can't provide, won't provide, or will not be providing in the future. Often the feeling will be anxiety, but anger, irritation, sadness, and general discomfort are all possibilities too.

These are not feelings to be 'healed', they are feelings to be taken seriously and acted upon responsibly.

The problem is that women tend to act upon these feelings in unhealthy and irresponsible ways that only exacerbate the problem rather than inspire the man to fix it. Here's some of the common ways:

1. She gaslights the feeling, downplays the feeling, justifies the feeling, or misattributes the feeling. The result is that she continues to go along with the mans lead, even though her instincts are telling her there is a serious problem. This will make it less likely that the man will provide because he feels less inspired to do so when his woman is communicating a lack of self-worth.

2. She communicates with reactivity, blame, or control. This triggers a man's instinct because she is disrespecting him, and that will begin to push him away. This will make it less likely that he will provide because a man loses inspiration to do so when his woman is disrespecting him rather than remaining open to receive him.

3. She steps up into the giving role doing more for him, hoping that if she gives enough he will see that she is worthy of being given to. This will also make it less likely that the man will provide because he feels less inspired to do so when his woman is communicating a lack of value.

Even though my wife's feminine instincts were suppressed, that didn't mean her instincts never gave her any warning that there was a problem before our son was born. Her instincts gave her tons of warnings.

About 4 months after meeting each other, we were planning on moving in together. I had left the city to work my driving job at a summer camp (yep, one more example of how I was still a boy, not a man). I left her the job of finding a suitable apartment for us to rent. I could have gotten it figured out before I left for the summer, but I didn't. I hadn't even considered it. I didn't see it as my role. I thought: "Why should I have to do it when my (at the time) girlfriend could?"

But finding an apartment is a man's job. It is part of being in the 'giving' role. Women are fully capable of doing it, but all of that planning and decision making is stressful on a woman's physiology. It's a gift that she needs to receive from a man to be able to relax. He finds / builds / buys the place to live, she turns it into a home.

We had a phone call when I was on the job picking up orders at my camp, because she wanted to know some things so she could make decisions about the apartment. Really what she wanted was for me to relieve her of the burden of making the decisions. But I didn't have answers and I wasn't taking her need for my leadership seriously. She got angry at me, and her anger resulted in me getting angry back at her. The call ended in one of our first arguments. I finished the call by telling her that she needed to figure it out herself.

At the time, and for years afterward, I couldn't understand why she was giving me such a hard time. I was working, and whatever she chose didn't matter to me.

At the time, she couldn't explain (logically) why she gave me such a hard time.

But it's clear now. She gave me a hard time because I was passively in the receiving role. I wasn't stepping up as the provider to take care of business and provide her with an apartment. I didn't see it as my role, I didn't care, I didn't see the burden it was putting on her as long as I was paying for my half of it. My wife was and is an incredibly competent woman. From my perspective, she was fully capable of doing it herself. Back then, I thought traditional gender roles were silly and unnecessary. Boy do I have egg on my face now.

One of the issues women have with doing this work is they identify with being strong and capable. They struggle with receiving from a man because having a man help them and take care of them conflicts with their identity. To make matters worse, men often reaffirm this identity by encouraging a woman to be strong and capable, or by letting her do too much. But that identity is a wound and doesn't serve a woman.

Yes ladies, you might be fully capable of carrying a big jug of water by yourself or finding your own solution to a problem. But the more you lead yourself with a man, the more you lose out on the joy of receiving his care, and the more he loses out on the joy of you receiving his care.

It's perfectly ok for a woman to be capable of anything. It's even ok for a woman to be just as good as a man at things. I like knowing that my wife could do a reasonable job taking care of herself if I died because she is so capable.

But gender roles do matter while we are interacting with each other because men need to be in the giving role and women need to be in the receiving role. This doesn't change even if the woman is so capable that she doesn't require help, advice, or support. She 'could' do it on her own, but she can't do it on her own and stay feminine, and she can't if she wants a happy man. Without being in these proper roles, problems, arguments, hurt feelings, loss of attraction, and unmet needs are guaranteed.

The issue for my wife and I was that she was stuck in the giving role because I had chosen the receiver role. Her instincts were telling her it was a problem. My instincts were too suppressed to see anything as a problem.

If I had understood why this role reversal was such an issue I could have averted almost all of the dozens of arguments we had throughout our relationship. But I didn't understand it, and unfortunately for women, most men today don't understand it either.

Nor will they choose to understand it if a woman tries to explain it to them, or even if a woman shows them this book (with only rare exception). That's just the way men are. This leaves women in a predicament. They struggle with not receiving the provision they need because their man isn't firmly in the giving role. But they don't know what to do about it.

You're about to learn what to do about it. A man will learn how to be in the giving role when a woman activates his instincts to be there. Let's talk about how to do that.

CHAPTER 4

FEMININE COMMUNICATION

Many women have a fantasy where it is unnecessary for them to express their needs or desires to a man. The man is so competent and in-tune with her feelings that he anticipates exactly what she needs and wants before she even knows. She fantasizes about him being a mind-reader.

He gives her hugs and kisses all day.

He plans amazing dates and time with her.

He helps her with opening jars and doors, lifting heavy objects, and cleaning up when she's stressed.

He buys thoughtful gifts for her all the time.

He gives her compliments and support whenever she's feeling down and gives her the perfect advice to help her feel good again.

All without her needing to say anything. He just knows what she needs.

This fantasy is very much aligned with the feminine instinct to receive. A woman feels the most cherished when she doesn't have to express her needs but they get met anyway.

This was a topic of conversation my wife and I had well after I had begun helping her let go of control to receive my gifts. Prior to the conversation, I had spent the previous few weeks overwhelmed in my business, working twelve plus hour days trying to manage a team and dozens of clients. Our second child (a girl) had recently been born, and I was also choosing to do more around the house and interacting with her to take some of the burden off my wife.

This took a huge toll on my energy and inspiration to give my wife affection and spend time with her. I started to withdraw and spent almost all free time by myself. My wife began to feel increasingly bad and started telling herself stories that she was doing something wrong. Until finally she asked to talk with me and shared that she felt sad.

She told me that she wanted me to initiate time and affection with her, without her needing to ask for that time and affection. She had little problem asking me to help her with something, but asking for affection was very different for her. She doesn't enjoy asking, because she doesn't want to be a burden and doesn't want to seem needy. Receiving affection when she asks for it doesn't feel nearly as good to her as receiving it when she doesn't have to ask. That's why she took so long to say something.

Here's the problem with that mindset:

For a woman, not being in the receiving role always boils down to self worth, in one way or another. When I refer to self worth for women, I am always referring to 'feminine' self worth. This is much different than masculine self worth. When a man has high masculine self worth, he knows that his job is to be in the giving role, and he knows that he deserves to have his gifts received and respected. He acts accordingly by leading his woman to receive him. Whereas when a woman has high feminine self worth, she knows that her job is to be in the receiving role, and she knows that she deserves to be cherished with a man's gifts. She also acts accordingly.

If a woman is in the receiving role and being cherished every day by a man, that is all well and good. She just follows his lead and receives his love and care. She's in her worth and acting accordingly. Easy.

The problem is, few women experience anything like that, and if a woman isn't experiencing that, she must learn how to communicate her needs in a feminine way that a man is inspired by.

A woman who is always in her feminine self worth will communicate her needs and desires when a man fails to anticipate them. She knows she feels best if her man anticipates her needs, but she knows she deserves better than to wait around feeling bad because her man isn't meeting those needs. If her needs aren't being met, she communicates freely.

If she doesn't communicate her needs when a man doesn't anticipate them, she's automatically demonstrating low self worth because she is tolerating a dynamic where her needs are not met. A woman with low self worth will be compelled into low self worth behavior such as avoidance and inhibition which is likely to create a self-fulfilling prophecy where her man treats her as unworthy because he isn't inspired. See how that works?

When she begins communicating her needs in a feminine way, she begins shifting into her feminine self worth because she's communicating that she is worthy of those needs being addressed. As she gets better at communicating and her self worth begins shifting, two things happen:

1. Her man starts to better understand her needs because she's frequently communicating them.

2. Her man is inspired to do a better job at anticipating her needs because he can feel her self worth.

By getting good at communicating her needs, a woman shifts her self worth over time. Communicating needs is the ultimate affirmation to God (or to the universe, take your pick) that you are worthy of having those needs met. The more you move through the discomfort and fear of doing it, the more worthy you will start to feel. Especially when your communication inspires a man into the giving role to give you what you need.

The more that a woman communicates her needs, the more she gets those needs met. The more she gets those needs met, the more that she realizes she is worthy of having those needs met. The more she realizes she is worthy, the more worthy she feels. The more worthy she feels, the more her man is inspired to anticipate her needs without her saying anything.

Eventually, the shift in a woman's self worth and communication creates her fantasy dynamic with a man where she rarely communicates those needs. Pretty cool, yes?

But there are no shortcuts, the only way to create that fantasy where a man anticipates almost every need sustainably in a long-term relationship is by getting good at communicating those needs.

If she needs help, she communicates.

If she needs affection, she communicates.

If she needs more time with her man, she communicates.

If she needs reassurance, she communicates.

If she needs direction or advice, she communicates.

But for this communication to inspire a positive response and natural desire to meet her needs, a woman must only communicate those needs with respect. Respect to a man doesn't look the same as respect for a woman. Most women unintentionally disrespect men by not knowing how to communicate. A man is inspired to be in the giving role only when he is communicated to with respect, and he is demotivated from that role when he is not.

To communicate with respect, a woman must not energetically lead her man. Which means she must not try to get an outcome with him. She can want an outcome, she can need an outcome, but there is a difference between wanting or needing an outcome, versus trying to get one.

For example, I could write this book to try to get praise, money, and to help people. Those are all outcomes. If I tried to get those outcomes, I'm leading towards them, and I'm in my masculine energy. If I write the book for the praise and money, I'm energetically taking. If I do it to help, I'm energetically giving (in the giving role), even though I will likely get some amount of money and praise in return. Both trying to take and trying to give are energetically masculine, because both are trying to get an outcome. When a woman operates in that energy with her man, it's a form of disrespect and communicates a lack of trust.

But let's say I wrote this book because it is my Truth from my heart that I need to share with the world. I share that Truth because I need to express, I need to get it on paper. Not because I'm trying to get any outcome from readers, but just to express. Just like a sculptor needs to express with clay, or a dancer needs to express with movement. Such an artist (if they are truly doing art) isn't trying to be understood or seen, nor are they trying to get their next paycheque. They can want such outcomes, but when they are doing their art, they are doing it only for the sake of expressing. When a person is expressing just to express, they are in the receiving role.

Expression puts a woman in the receiving role because in that energetic state, she is controlling nothing. When she stops trying to get an outcome, she stops trying to control the world externally. If she stops trying to control the world, she is opening herself to receive whatever the world chooses to give her. If she's expressing in this energy with a man, she is choosing to be receptive to whatever gift he chooses to give her, if any.

When a woman communicates in this way, she is using what I call 'feminine communication'. Feminine communication is permissive, vulnerable, and does not try to get outcomes. It also inspires a man to step into the giving role to meet her needs, when she uses it to express those needs.

Here are a few examples of feminine communication that a woman can use:

ASKING PERMISSION - When you ask a question permissively, you are not leading. You are not trying to get an outcome. You are asking permission for an outcome. Energetically, you are opening yourself up to receive a man's leadership. Either by granting permission or denying it. Feel into the energy of being permissive. Notice how it helps you shift out of trying to control and lead. It's not the words that are important so much as the energy that the words naturally help you shift into. The words help you let go of control. It helps you shift into the receiving role, so that you can receive.

"Can I have some time with you?"

"Can I have a hug?"

"May I have some advice?"

"May I get something to eat now?"

"May I have some help with the baby?"

"May I share my feelings?" (this one is especially important)

FEELINGS – When you share your feelings vulnerably, you aren't trying to get an outcome. You are sharing your emotional experience. You are doing it for you, because you need to share. Focus on feeling the feeling as you say it. You are tapping into your unmet need by feeling the feeling. Share only the feeling, as an "I feel statement." Have faith that your feelings matter to him. Have faith in his desire to understand you and help you. Have faith that he will lead further to understand why you feel this way.

"I feel sad."

"I feel angry."

"I feel anxiety."

"I feel overwhelm."

"I feel hungry."

Before sharing your feelings, ask permission to share ("May I / Can I share what I am feeling?"). The reason you must ask permission is not because you don't have the right to speak, this is not about oppression, this is not about being 'less than'. What you are really asking for is to have space held for you which requires a man's time, energy, and presence. You are not entitled to that, and if you believe you are, a man will never want to give it to you as a gift. If you are sharing your feelings about unmet needs, a man will need to be in a place to consider you. Once a man grants permission, share the feeling that is being brought up because of the unmet need.

PROBLEMS/NEEDS – When you share problems or needs, you aren't trying to get an outcome. You are sharing because you need to express. You aren't expressing those problems with blame and judgment (which is disrespectful) and are instead sharing those problems vulnerably. What you are essentially doing when you are sharing these problems is opening yourself to receive a man's solution.

"Because I'm struggling to take care of the kids alone."

"Because I didn't get to see you last week."

"Because I didn't get any kisses yesterday."

"Because I'm not receiving as many compliments as before and I start telling myself stories that I'm not good enough for you."

"Because I paid for our date."

When he asks you why you feel that way, tell him as factually as you can the problem you are experiencing without any value judgments. Stick to the objective facts. Also try to personalize the problem by focusing on your unmet need, rather than focusing on why his behavior isn't good enough to meet that need. Notice the examples of problems start with "I" rather than with "you".

For you to ask and open to receive his solution, where do you need to be? The receiving role.

For him to hold space and provide you with his solution, where does he need to be? The giving role.

By you shifting into feminine energy when using feminine communication, you create a dynamic where the man ends up in the giving role. You didn't tell him or lead him to be there, because that will never work. He shifted there because you shifted yourself into the receiving role. You focused on yourself, rather than on what he needs to do.

YOU: ***"Zak, May I share a feeling?"*** – permissive

ME: *"Yes go ahead."*

YOU: ***"I feel confusion."*** – feeling

ME: *"Tell me why you feel that way."*

YOU: ***"Because I don't know what this communication would look like in practice."*** – problem

ME: *"Reflect on this made up exchange, it is your first example of what this would look like in practice. There will be many more."*

Spend a moment feeling into this example of an exchange.

Who would be the one leading? Who would be the one in control and in charge? Who would be the one giving time, energy, help, and love? That's right, me, the man. Even though you started the conversation.

Who would be following the lead? Who would be the one who is letting go of control? Who would be the one opening up to receive time, energy, help, and love? That's right, you, the woman.

If you were to have this conversation you would be putting yourself into the receiving role, and making it extremely easy for a man (in this case, me) to be in the giving role to lead you and give you whatever you need. You would be inspiring the man to want to help you and meet your needs, because you are communicating respect, receptivity, and self-worth.

Contrast this with saying nothing and hoping you get what you need.

Also contrast it with leading the conversation where you feel tense and unnatural because you aren't energetically letting go and are instead 'trying' to make the conversation go somewhere to get something from a man.

Feminine communication is a massive topic. So massive, that I could write dozens of books on it but they would still only scratch the surface of feminine communication. That's because feminine communication is as rich a language as Spanish or English or Mandarin. But unlike those languages, feminine communication is fully dependent on the energy behind the words. It takes months of support in our 'Relationship Of Your Dreams Academy" for women to begin to be fluent in it. This chapter is a greatly condensed and simplified outline of what feminine communication is, what it can look like, and why to use it.

While I will be providing many examples of feminine communication throughout this book to illustrate how to get a man to help you into the receiving role (without trying), I will not be going into detail about what feminine communication looks like or why it works because that is not the focus of this book. The focus is on learning how to receive.

If you want to learn more about using feminine communication, read my other books, book a spot for our masterclass, and consider working with us in 'Relationship Of Your Dreams Academy'. You can find links to all of those resources on my website www.relationshipofyourdreams.com.

With that out of the way, what I have given you above is a good starting point so that you can use this book to do 3 things:

1. Shift into the receiving role energetically when expressing an unmet need.

2. Communicate your need to a man so he knows what it is and becomes inspired to find a solution to meet it.

3. Ask for help in shifting a pattern where you are stuck in control and are having difficulty receiving.

You have been given a basic intro of number 1 and 2 in this chapter.

Number 3 is what we will be focusing on for the remainder of this book.

I will show you what patterns you are in that are demotivating a man/men from giving you what you need.

I will show you why you are stuck in those patterns.

I will show you how to start shifting those patterns when with a man.

Finally, I will show you how to ask a man for help to assist you in shifting the pattern. Don't believe you need to shift these patterns on your own. It's impossible. Trying to do it alone would also ironically be going against what you're learning in this book, which is to inspire a man to give you what you need by being open to receive from him. You need a man's help to stay in the receiving role because you will fail to do it on your own without help. Trust me.

CHAPTER 5

HOW TO STOP GIVING

The first (and most obvious) way that a woman fails to stay in the receiving role is by stepping right into the giving role. A woman is in the giving role whenever she anticipates a man's needs, or whenever she tries to get her needs met by initiating instead of asking permission for what she needs.

There are many things a woman could do to step into the giving role. My dating and relationship life has provided me with endless examples. Here's a few of the ways I have experienced:

Women drove me around in their cars.

Women paid for meals on dates.

Women paid for and even surprised me with comedy shows, sex shows, etc.

Women planned and took me on vacation getaways.

Women would surprise me with little gifts.

Women bought me clothes.

Women would initiate cuddling, handholding, kissing, etc.

Women would clean my house.

Women would compliment me on my looks, my jokes, my personality.

What makes these above examples especially problematic was that these things were usually done without me telling these women to do any of it. It was of their own initiative. They were anticipating what I would like or love to make me happy.

"But didn't you like women being so thoughtful and showing you how much they liked you?"

Yes I did. When my masculine instincts were suppressed, I did like it because the perks received were more important to me than the responsibility of being in my natural role. It made my life easier and I got free stuff and free services. I did enjoy the validation of being so awesome that a woman would do this stuff for me. But it didn't make me feel any closer to those women. It didn't create attraction. It didn't make me want to claim them exclusively (about half of the time women would do these things for me outside of relationships). It didn't make me love them more. Most importantly, it didn't inspire me to be in the giving role. Just the opposite. It inspired me to lean back and be even lazier.

Today, if my wife were to do any of these things for me, not only would it not inspire me, I would feel irritation. My instincts are fully online, and they warn me when she even slightly slips into the giving role. I feel less joy when this happens than if she were to do nothing, because I don't need to receive from her, I only need her to receive from me.

That doesn't mean a woman should never do anything for a man, but it does mean if she's doing something for a man, it should only be because he led her to do it. If it's through his leadership, he's in the giving role giving her his leadership. If she follows his leadership, he will feel received and respected, and thus inspired to Devote to her.

But when a woman does things for a man by anticipating his needs rather than following his leadership, she's in the giving role and he's in the receiving role. That will cause problems and increasingly demotivate a man from wanting to be in the giving role.

Is this a little confusing? Let's simplify.

If I tell my wife to make me a sandwich and she follows that leadership by making me one, I'm in the giving role, she's in the receiving role. I feel received (respected) when she follows my direction.

But if my wife anticipates that I want a sandwich and makes it for me as a surprise, she's in the giving role, I'm in the receiving role. I don't feel received. Though I may enjoy the sandwich.

A second example:

If I tell my wife to come over and give me a massage after a long day at work and she follows that leadership by giving me a massage, I'm in the giving role, she's in the receiving role. I feel received (respected) when she follows my direction.

But if she anticipates that I want a massage and comes over and starts massaging me, she's in the giving role, I'm in the receiving role. I don't feel received. Though I may enjoy the massage.

There are two main ways a woman can be in the giving role; initiating and mothering.

Initiating is when both man and woman would benefit from the gift. When a woman initiates by being in the giving role she is taking away the man's opportunity to serve her.

For example, my wife and I would both benefit from hand holding because I enjoy holding her hand and she enjoys holding my hand. But if my wife were to grab my hand when we are walking side-by-side, she would take away my opportunity to give her the gift of me taking her hand to hold it. I would have felt good by giving her that small act of love, but if she initiated, I can no longer give it to her in that moment.

Another example; my wife and I would both benefit from spending time together doing something because we enjoy spending time together. But if my wife were to make plans to go to the movies with me, or to watch a movie with me at home, she took away my opportunity to make those plans for her as a gift. I would have felt good planning that for her, but if she initiated, I can no longer do that for her.

Mothering is a bit different, the gift is more one-sided. When a woman mothers, she is doing something that primarily benefits the man. At least, in theory. But in practice, it's not benefitting him because it's not giving him the opportunity to step up and lead and heal his wounds.

For example, if I was trying to put on my daughter's diaper, and my wife starts to give me advice to do it better, that is mothering. She is trying to help, but if I didn't need help, she is interfering. If I did need help, she took away my opportunity to lead her to assist me. We would have both felt good if I led her to help me, but if she tries to help without me leading her to, neither of us feel good.

Another example, if I was very busy at work and we were going on a trip, and my wife decides to pack my suitcase to save me time, that is mothering. She is trying to help, but it's interfering if I didn't lead her to help. If I did need help because I was swamped with work, she again took away my opportunity to lead her to assist me.

If I told her *"Come show me how to put on this diaper properly."* Or *"Babe, I'm busy with work, pack my suitcase for me, thankyou."* then I would remain in the giving role because I'm giving her my leadership, and she would remain in the receiving role because she's receiving that leadership. I would feel inspired to serve her more because she is receiving me, and I would feel received.

One of my ex-girlfriends in my 20's was a giver and she did lots of initiating and mothering. I'm going to use her as an example of what not to do, because my wife has never been much of a giver in this way. I had often compelled my wife into the giver role because I was frequently stubbornly stuck in the receiver role due to being very passive, but only rarely was she there because she wanted to be.

My ex-girlfriend though, wanted to be there. She was a very happy, exuberant, fun, silly, flirty woman. She had many amazing feminine qualities. The one masculine quality she had was that she was a giver. She was in the giving role a lot with me. She would initiate spending time together, she'd buy me things, she'd compliment me, she'd do things for me without me asking, and she'd get into my physical space and touch me, a lot.

Again, for many readers, this might sound great. On one level, it is great to be liked and valued that much. It's great to be validated. But it isn't what a man needs, even if he likes it on some level. Because she was in the giving role, she ensured that I would never feel inspired to step into the giving role to cherish her.

One time, she invited me to go to a restaurant, her treat. I accepted. She drove us in her car (because I didn't drive and didn't have a car). We sat, we ordered, she paid. But none of it felt 'right.' Here was this amazing woman with a lot of feminine qualities who values me a lot, yet I could have ended it with her at any time and I'd be completely fine.

I enjoyed my time with her, I felt enough attraction to her to enjoy having sex with her. But there was no strong 'pull'. There was no desire from me to want to take care of her or make her feel special. I had no interest in anything long-term with her, I couldn't see any future, and I had little attachment. I started taking her for granted, as I gradually wanted to see her less often. Eventually, I broke up with her. Her being in the giving role wasn't the only reason the relationship didn't work out, but it was a big part of it.

This is something women struggle to understand. Why would being so kind and loving result in getting so little kindness and loving back? Was it because I was a narcissist? Was it because I was deeply damaged? Was it because I was emotionally unavailable?

No. It was because I was (and still am) a man. Men do not appreciate a woman being in the giving role, and they will never be inspired to be better men when a woman is there. The reason why is because our masculine instinct is wired to not value a woman when she is giving. It doesn't fulfill a man's need, because a man receiving from a woman doesn't increase his chances of his genes surviving, it decreases it. From an instinctual standpoint, he only has a need to be received.

We will talk again about our cave people friends to understand more about the masculine instinct so you can understand why men do not need to receive from a woman.

Let's say Fred and Wilma have that wild night on their honeymoon and Wilma ends up getting pregnant. But instead of Wilma staying warm inside the cave as she grows her baby inside her, she starts going out and doing things for Fred. She tells him to relax and watch cave-people TV, while she provides and protects him.

Maybe that sounds great to some men on a conceptual level. But there is a problem: Cave-people are instinctually wired for survival. If Wilma stressed herself out providing for him, would that help or hurt the survival chance of his genes?

It would hurt them. Of course. So Fred might enjoy being lazy on some level while his woman provides for him. Cave-people TV is fantastic. But he is not wired to enjoy receiving from Wilma because it doesn't help the chances of his genes surviving, it will hurt them.

To be clear; this hypothetical probably didn't occur with our ancient ancestors. Cave-people have not had their instincts suppressed or covered over with wounding and social conditioning to make them behave in such unnatural ways like modern-women do. If any cave-ladies did behave this way, their genes would very quickly die out and be removed from the gene pool. That's why we only have instincts today that motivate people to conform to their gender roles; where males provide, females are provided for.

But modern society allows us the 'luxury' of being very wounded generation after generation and still manage to procreate. Men with online masculine instincts will begin to lose interest in a woman the more that she gives. But a wounded man might like all the stuff a woman buys for him or does for him without telling her to do it. He might like her setting up plans and giving him advice. If a man is very wounded, he might even feel validated on a superficial level when his woman does that or if she compliments him or gives him hugs or support. But that's his wounding being validated. His instincts don't want it. He may stick around and even enjoy her anticipating his needs, but he will never heal from those wounds and become her provider and protector if she continues to stay in the giving role with him.

It doesn't matter if a man hasn't had sex with the woman yet. It doesn't matter if she isn't pregnant with his child. These instincts don't just become factors when certain conditions are met (though they often become greatly heightened when certain conditions are met). The instincts are always part of a man, to his core. It defines a man more than anything else. He doesn't need to receive from a woman. He isn't wired for it because there is only a genetic cost to his offspring.

Women often believe that because they feel all gooey and special when a man gives things to them, that he will feel the same way when given to. He won't. In fact, the more it is done the more it will repel a man if his instinct is even remotely online. There is a huge inverse correlation between how much a woman gives to a man and how attracted he is to her. The more a woman gives, the less attracted he will tend to be. When giving is done excessively, women tend to not be claimed by men, or they tend to attract men who use them and don't step up. That loss of attraction and inspiration to Devote is our masculine instincts telling us that it is a poor decision to dedicate our time providing for the woman. Our instincts are telling us that our genes have a higher chance of survival if we claim a different woman who can receive.

When it's done infrequently, like giving gifts on birthdays and Christmas the overall detrimental effect will be significantly smaller, but it still won't help inspire a man into Devotion. My wife used to give me gifts very infrequently, a few small things a year. One time she got me a nighttime blindfold to help me sleep better. It was great. It was exactly what I needed. But I didn't feel 'loved' or 'special' because she was thinking of me. It didn't make me feel closer to her in any way. I didn't feel more attracted to her. I didn't 'need' to receive from her in that way, because I'm a man.

So if men are not wired to receive from a woman, how is it that so many women end up in the giving role? There's a few reasons for this, all of them are due to wounding.

1. The first reason a woman might be in the giving role is to manipulate a man into giving to her, or to not abandon her. This is 'giving to get'. From an energetic standpoint, a woman isn't truly in the giving role when she does this even though it may look like it on the surface. Truly energetic giving is only possible when a gift is given without any strings attached. It is done because she wants to show love. Think about this; when you are giving someone something like a Christmas gift, the most important thing you are giving is the love. The other person feels loved, because you are doing it without trying to get something. The only reason to do that is because you love to see them happy.

Whereas giving to get is energetically taking. There is no love that is given, and so if the other person senses the manipulation, they will not feel loved. They will not feel validated. Sure they got the 'thing'. But the 'thing' wasn't what they really needed. They needed the love.

2. The second reason a woman might be in the giving role is because the man put her there. A man could put her there through his passivity, for example, by not taking charge to plan any dates. Or he could put her there by leading her to be there, for example, by telling her to pay for some or all of dates. These situations will only put a woman in the giving role superficially. Energetically, she isn't truly there, because she isn't operating from a place of love. She will 'give' from a place of irritation, guilt, or fear (feelings which may be buried and not consciously felt). It will be obligatory 'giving', and that is not giving.

3. The third reason a woman might be in the giving role is because she believes her value comes from what she can do for or give to a man. If she has this belief she will be compelled into this role so that she will feel valuable. This could be because of shame, but it could also come from a self-validating place. A woman self-validates in this way where she tries to feel 'good enough' by being in the giving role. It's not for the man though, it's for her own self-validation to feel worthy. To energetically be in the giving role, the gift must be given with love.

4. The fourth reason a woman might be in the giving role is because she's truly doing it out of love. Energetically she truly is in the giving role. Think of the mother giving her child milk or comfort or toys out of love. That's real. She is in the giving role energetically, there is love that she is giving. But there is still a problem; men don't need a woman's love, little boys do. If a man is deeply wounded, he might think he needs to be loved this way. He might even feel good receiving love. But it's not what he needs at his core, and it will not inspire him into the giving role. It will keep him stuck in the receiving role.

All of these reasons have one important thing in common: The woman is being compelled into the giving role because of certain feelings she is feeling. This may be anxiety, but it may also be irritation, shame, or desire.

These feelings are ok to have. There are no wrong feelings, and there are no bad feelings. Feelings are perfect the way they are. If a woman tries to fight or suppress her feelings, she is waging war against herself, because her feelings are a part of her.

But the behaviors need to shift, so she can shift into the receiving role. Only once she is receiving a man, will he be inspired to step up into Devotion and cherish her.

To shift the behaviors, she needs help. Her man needs to know what she is feeling and why, so he can help her. Let's go back to my example I used with my ex-girlfriend. Almost certainly her behaviors in the giving role were motivated by anxiety and possibly shame. Anxiety of possibly losing me because she didn't believe she was good enough for me and shame when feeling that lack of self worth. She needed to use feminine communication with me to address the problem:

"May I share what I am feeling?"

"Yes."

"I feel anxiety and shame."

"Oh, why?"

"Because I don't believe I'm worthy of you in this moment. I buy

things for you so I feel worthy enough to be with you. But I'm really stuck.

This is a basic example of how a woman could share her feelings and the problem she is experiencing. The results you get by communicating in this way depend on how competent of a leader the man is, and on how activated his masculine instincts are. There is much more you could do if he doesn't immediately jump into problem solving mode and give you competent support. But this is a general idea of what this communication would look like to shift your patterns.

Understand that your job is not to solve the problem. You are asking for his help, and having faith that he will help you. That is how feminine communication works.

The alternative is summoning a ton of willpower and self-awareness to fight all of your old patterns alone. You would have to stop initiating everything, stop all mothering, stop all advice giving, stop planning, stop doing anything for him that he didn't tell you to do. Then deal with the emotional mess you become as you go against all of your patterns you've been stuck in your entire life. Think you are up for the task?

What are you going to do when your anxiety and guilt get stronger and you start telling yourself how selfish you are?

What are you going to do when the man starts complaining about how you don't do anything for him anymore?

What are you going to do when you start getting even less from a man as you get less, and then you panic thinking this can't work?

All of these things can happen, and all probably will. Unless you ask him for help so he understands what is going on and what you need.

It doesn't matter whether the man is your long-time husband or a first date, it is appropriate to ask for help if you notice your patterns are compelling you to give.

You are worthy of that help.

You are worthy to receive.

CHAPTER 6

HOW TO STOP RESISTING

The second way that a woman fails to stay in the receiving role is by resisting a man's gifts. That resistance can take several forms. She could suggest different gifts she wants instead ("how about we go to the movies instead?") she could judge his gifts ("this advice won't work"), or she could not accept his gifts and even set boundaries against them ("No I don't want to do that, I'm not going.").

Here are a few ways women have resisted my gifts:

Insisting paying for a date when I've tried to pay.

Saying "no" to, or making excuses to sex. (if this one triggers you, I understand, keep reading the chapter)

Telling me "I don't want to do that." when explaining a date night.

Arguing with me when I gave advice.

Getting upset when I've cleaned up to make a woman's life easier.

Luckily, my wife has provided ample examples of resisting my gifts to illustrate what this looks like, so we will be talking about her again. While she doesn't like being in the giving role, she has certainly resisted me trying to be there.

Prior to my masculine instincts coming online, I had invested a good chunk of time leading my wife to touch me more. Touching, and receiving touch did not come naturally to her for whatever reason, and I wanted to change that. I naturally love touch. I love to touch, and I love being touched. I am very affectionate and the number one way I used to enjoy showing my love is by giving my love through touch. Back then I also felt loved when I was being given touch. As long as it wasn't excessive, and with my wife, it wasn't.

That was why I had directed my wife to touch me more by initiating kissing and cuddling more. To play with my hair more. I reminded her frequently. I thought that this was what I needed, at the time, it felt like it.

After my instincts came online, I didn't want my wife to initiate touch anymore. It was like a switch went off, and my desire to receive love in this way completely disappeared. Whereas my need to give love in this way and have that love fully received became much stronger than it had ever been.

The problem was, my wife often resisted my touch. Either by making it clear she wasn't interested. Or, by not appearing to enjoy it. She didn't seem nearly as interested, grateful, or turned on as I needed her to be. She wasn't fully receiving me when I kissed her, hugged her, or held her.

She had always been that way. Before my instincts came online it didn't bother me much. However, once my instincts did come online, I felt horrible. Every time she resisted it felt like a rejection. I'm no stranger to rejection and I handle it well. But coming from my wife, especially with rejecting my touch of all things, it was an unpleasant experience. A man will feel bad when he tries to love his woman and it is not received. He may not visibly show it like a woman. He may not cry or start expressing feelings. But he feels that pain.

I've dated many women before my wife, and most were very visibly affected by my touch in a positive way. They loved it. Many couldn't get enough of it. They were fully 'receiving' it. Their reaction made me want to touch them much more. My joy was in my touch being received. But it was very different with my wife, at least outside of the bedroom. Even though she loved me, even though she was attracted to me.

There was a point after my instincts came online that I sat her down and had a conversation about this issue. This happened after I had just tried to kiss her while she was in the kitchen doing something during the start of cleaning day. She put up resistance and gave me an excuse that she was 'really busy'. Silly excuse of course, a kiss takes three seconds. For me, this was an issue that had to be solved, because the result of her resistance was that I became increasingly less motivated to give her physical affection.

From our conversation, I learned that she did want a lot of physical affection. She told me that she loves my touch, but for some reason unknown to her, she sometimes puts up resistance with an unconscious desire for me to fight through it. Unfortunately, the result was that her resistance only demotivated me and pushed me away. Even once I consciously understood that the resistance didn't mean she didn't want my touch, I still did not feel the inspiration to touch her often, because I often didn't feel received when I tried. I had to use willpower to continue helping her through the resistance until she became increasingly more receptive.

A woman needs to be given love. But a man needs to have his love received. When his gifts are not received, he is getting the message that he is not valued. That he is not good enough. That he is not worthy. That his gifts are undesired. Wounding can exacerbate how reactive a man is to this resistance, but it's his instinct that is warning him. My emotional reaction has ranged from a slight irritation, to deep sadness, to extreme anger, depending on what gift my wife was resisting and how she was resisting it.

We see why this is such a big deal to a man when we go back to the cave-people.

Let's say after Fred and Wilma consummate their wedding with amazing passionate cave-people sex, Wilma gets pregnant. Fred starts being a good husband and going out to bring back food for Wilma. Wilma doesn't want any of it.

The more she resists his provision, the higher the chance that his genetic offspring will be born undernourished and weak. Which means that his genes may die out. If this happened, his instincts would tell him that there is a problem, because Wilma is hurting his genes chance of survival. He needs her to receive his gifts to maximize his chance of gene survival.

But this goes even deeper. One form of provision is sex. A man gives his penis and sperm to his woman. For that gift to be received, she must sexually submit and be penetrated by the man. If Wilma resists and fights off Fred he won't be able to give his gift. Her not receiving his gift is a total genetic death sentence, because now he is unable to make offspring with her, and his genetic line ends with him if he doesn't find another mate. Again, his instincts will warn him that there is a problem.

If Fred were to stay with and continue to provide resources to Wilma when she doesn't receive those resources, he'd be wasting his time from a gene survival perspective because there's a good chance his offspring won't survive.

But if Fred were to stay with and continue to provide resources to Wilma when she doesn't even sexually receive him, he'd be wasting his time from a gene survival perspective because there's a 100% chance his offspring will never be born. This sets off every instinctual alarm bell Fred has.

In both cases, his instincts will tell him that his genes will die out, because he is providing gifts to someone who is not interested in receiving from him. Those instincts cause a feeling of irritation when resistance is experienced, and eventually the levels of attraction and interest he has for Wilma will plummet. His instincts tell him, "Don't stick around, don't provide, leave her, find someone else to give to who will receive you."

That is why men are so sensitive when a woman judges his gifts, when she creates boundaries against his gifts, or when she rejects his gift and suggests something else. It doesn't have to be sex or food his woman isn't receiving. It's any gift. Even though many of the things men give a woman do not directly impact gene survival if she doesn't receive it, it doesn't matter. Our instincts don't know any difference and warn us anyway. Those instincts are telling a man: "Don't stick around, don't provide, leave her, find someone else to give to who will receive you."

Men are unlikely to leave a woman the first time she doesn't receive his gifts. The masculine instinct is persistent, so a man is not likely to give up after one attempt unless he has some serious emotional wounding on top of those instincts or wasn't very attracted to the woman in the first place. But every time a woman resists, even a little, a man loses a little more inspiration to be in the giving role and cherish her. Eventually, if the resistance is frequent and extreme enough, he will give up. Only very wounded men would continue to attempt to provide for a woman who doesn't receive his sexual and/or non-sexual gifts.

Most women have probably experienced this issue more than once with sex. Rejecting a man when he leads to have sex is one of the most instinct activating things she could do. The reason why is outlined in the cave-people example. If a woman communicates that she doesn't want her man's sperm, even if she has had sex with him many times before, his instincts tell him that he has no genetic reason to devote to her. Instincts don't understand birth control, nor do they understand headaches. A man's instincts simply react to a woman who resists his gifts.

You can't win against a man's instincts. You can't fight them. You can only seek to understand them and work with those instincts, to receive what you want and need. To do that, you need to learn why you are working against his instincts by resisting his gifts. There are several reasons a woman would resist:

1. She doesn't feel worthy of his gifts. A woman with low self worth will struggle to receive all of a man's gifts, because deep down, she doesn't believe she deserves them. She might think she does conceptually, but due to woundings, she unconsciously believes she deserves little and her behaviors reflect that. A woman who lacks self worth in this way tends to feel shame or even anxiety when receiving 'too much'. That blocks her gratitude, and compels her into insisting that the gift is not necessary, or into suggesting something else. If you have ever told a man he shouldn't have spent that much on you, or if you argue with him when he says you're beautiful, this is stemming from low self worth.

2. She believes she is entitled to better gifts. A woman who has been wounded often has entitlement problems, believing that she is 'owed' something from the world and from a man. On the surface, entitlement might look like self worth because a woman is communicating she deserves something. But in reality it's pointing to parts of herself that she has cut off and stopped loving and accepting. When a woman judges gifts or blames a man for not giving better ones, there is entitlement present.

3. She lacks trust in a man to take care of her and consider her feelings and needs, which often is also related to self worth issues. So when a man tries to give a gift that is mis-timed or not appropriate (or that she perceives as such), she will resist with walls, boundaries, and suggestions instead of using feminine communication to share the problem or her feelings.

In all three of these examples, a woman's lack of self worth creates a self-fulfilling prophecy by compelling her into resistant behaviors which eventually push the man away or causes him to lose his inspiration. Thus giving her evidence to confirm her deepest beliefs that she deserves little. In these examples, she literally cannot receive a man's gift because she is being blocked by feelings of anxiety, shame, or irritation.

I will be addressing number 1 and 2 in much more detail in a later chapter, but for the remainder of this chapter, I will be focusing on reason number 3. Number 3 is by far the most important from an emotional safety and physical safety perspective. A woman often resists not just because a gift is unwanted, but also because the gift may be hurting her in some way.

It may sound strange to talk about 'gifts' hurting a person, but this is common.

For example, when a man is leading a woman to sex when she has a horrible headache and brutal period cramps, the sex is a gift, but it is a mis-timed gift.

Or if a woman has been traumatized by clowns, taking her to a circus for a date is a gift, but it is an inappropriate gift.

Or, if a woman has been traumatized by clowns and has a headache with period cramps, a man leading her to sex while dressed in a clown outfit could in some alternate reality be considered a gift, but it is certainly a mistimed and inappropriate one due to the circumstances. The choice in gift may also suggest the man needs a therapist. Either way, a woman would understandably be compelled into resisting such a 'gift' with a boundary.

But much of the time, unwanted gifts are not quite as extreme.

What does a woman do when a man tries to give her the gift of his time but she's exhausted and needs to sleep?

What does a woman do when a man tries to give her the gift of sexualized compliments but it's a first date and she isn't ready for that?

What does a woman do when a man tries to give her the gift of helping her clean up but he's just getting in her way and making her job more difficult?

In these situations where a gift is unwanted, a woman would be dishonoring her heart and her needs to say nothing and stay open to receive these gifts. The man needs to know that there is a problem with receiving the gift. Pretending to love what he's giving you when you will feel bad is not healthy, nor is it going to inspire him. But resisting the gift will trigger his instinct and he will lose Devotion. What is the solution?

The solution, regardless of why that resistance is coming up, is to use feminine communication. Underneath that resistance there is always a feeling, usually it will be anxiety, shame, or irritation. Most of the time it is best to start by sharing that.

I will use an example of a man trying to kiss a woman on a first date but she isn't ready yet.

"May I share what I am feeling?"

"Yes."

"I feel very anxious."

"Why?"

"Because I really like you but I haven't had a man try to kiss me this soon. I don't know if I am ready."

"Oh. Ok no problem we don't have to kiss yet until you feel more comfortable with me."

Pay very close attention here. What happened in this exchange is very different than if the woman just said "No I'm not ready yet."

If a woman were to say "No I'm not ready yet." she is in her masculine energy resisting a man's gift. She's not in the receiving role because she's leading by setting her own boundary. She's giving the man her boundary to protect herself, which puts her in the giving role and him back in the receiving role receiving the boundary.

Whereas in the initial communication example, the woman doesn't resist or set a boundary. She shares her feelings, and when prompted she shares the problem she is experiencing. This inspires the man to lead, and set a temporary boundary for himself. He is giving the woman the gift of creating boundaries for himself so she can feel comfortable before getting more physical. This time, he makes the choice rather than her. He is giving her leadership that considers her needs.

This isn't just a form of provision, it's also a form of protection. When a woman communicates in this respectful way, it inspires a man to protect her heart, from himself and his own inconsiderate, irresponsible, or incompetent decisions. The protection instinct is incredibly powerful. It is the same instinct that was on full alert when I was trying to help my son Mikah at the hospital. There is nothing more natural for a man than feeling a deep sense of responsibility for his woman's physical AND emotional protection, when she communicates in a way that activates his instincts.

If you use feminine communication you may not be receiving a man's specific gift that he initially wanted to give you because he decides the gift isn't the right thing to give. At least, not in that moment. But you are still receiving his leadership, which is also a gift. Instead of pushing him away by disrespecting him with your resistance, you'll be respecting him with your receptivity to his lead. In the above example, you didn't resist his gift, energetically. You told him a problem you were experiencing while trusting his leadership. You communicated trust and respect, which is a form of receptivity. After he understood the problem, he rejected his own gift, realizing it was inappropriate, and gave you a different gift that was more appropriate for the situation.

A man shouldn't always set boundaries for himself when a woman is uncomfortable or not wanting a certain gift. In my earlier example with my wife resisting my kisses, me setting a boundary for myself to not kiss her wouldn't be helping either of us. What she really needed was to be lovingly led through her resistance and whatever feelings were causing it.

"May I share what I am feeling?"

"Yes."

"I feel sad."

"Why do you feel sad?"

"Because I continue to resist your kisses. I don't mean to. It's an automatic reaction. I need help, I don't know how to work on this."

"Oh. Thankyou for telling me, I didn't understand why you didn't seem to enjoy being kissed. I'm going to help you through your resistance."

This brings up the nuance of resistance and boundaries. I can't tell you how many times a woman (including my wife) set boundaries that was not serving her. The boundaries were there not because they were healthy boundaries, but because of wounding compelling her into controlling something that didn't need to be controlled. Often blocking her ability to receive.

Some women even set boundaries to stop men from paying for

their meals on dates. They don't want to feel like they 'owe' a man anything and see it as empowering to pay for themselves. If you have gotten this far in the book, you probably aren't that kind of woman (or if you are, you don't want to be that kind of woman anymore). But you may resist or set boundaries to prevent receiving other gifts that you should be receiving. You need a man's help to be led through that resistance. So stop setting boundaries and instead use feminine communication to ask for that help so you can shift into the receiving role.

If that directive has you wondering what to do when a man doesn't protect your heart even when you use feminine communication, don't worry, I cover that in the next chapter.

CHAPTER 7

HOW TO STOP COMPLYING

The third way that a woman fails to stay in the receiving role is by 'receiving' gifts when she doesn't truly want them or may hurt her in some way to receive them. We just finished talking about resisting gifts as an unhealthy pattern, but now we will discuss the flip side as an equally unhealthy pattern.

When a woman chooses to receive gifts that she doesn't want or may have a negative impact on her, she is dishonoring her heart. To better understand what I am referring to, we are going to talk about 'submission'.

The word 'submit' (in the context I use it) is synonymous with the word 'receive'. A woman 'submits' to all of a man's gifts. She submits to his touch, to his gifts, to his plans and decisions, to his sex, to his support, to his leadership. Naturally, for a woman to submit to a man's gifts, that means the man has to be leading to give those gifts.

Which means that we can now explain a man and woman's core needs from earlier in this book in a different way. A woman needs a man to lead (so she can be cherished) and a man needs a woman to submit to his lead (so he can be received).

The word 'submission' has unfortunately picked up some negative connotations. Making people think of BDSM and / or being treated like a slave when they hear it. There is nothing wrong with some of that in the bedroom when playing pretend, but healthy women don't want to be treated as a slave throughout a relationship.

When women think of the word 'submission' they often think it makes a woman 'less than' and 'inferior to' a man. But this is not true if the man is leading her with Devotion and considering her needs as important as his own.

Some of the time in a healthy relationship a woman will be submitting to leadership that directly benefits her. For example, when a man tells her to get ready for an amazing dinner date, or when a man buys her a gift. A healthy man will enjoy giving his woman things and experiences, even if only she benefits. His joy is from pleasing his woman with his leadership.

Other times in a healthy relationship a woman will be submitting to leadership that benefits both her and him roughly equally. For example, submitting to holding hands, or submitting to his direction to cuddle up to him on the couch while watching a movie. A healthy man will enjoy giving/leading, and a healthy woman will enjoy receiving/submitting in this way when they both benefit.

But being in the receiving role does not mean a woman does nothing for a man. It doesn't mean that the man must work his butt off all day constantly anticipating his woman's needs while she gets manicures and goes shoe shopping. Such a dynamic will not inspire a man's Devotion because it would be non-reciprocal. The only way to inspire Devotion is to fully receive him, which means submitting to his leadership. That includes submitting to leadership that fulfills his needs and desires, not just receiving leadership that fulfills hers.

There will be times where she will be submitting to leadership that primarily or exclusively is for the benefit of him. For example, when he directs her to give him a blowjob or make him a sandwich. Or when he sets the expectation that she is in charge of cooking and cleaning. A healthy woman will enjoy submitting to her man even if only he tangibly benefits, because her joy is from pleasing her man through her submission. Assuming of course that she is submitting to a man who is Devotional and considering her needs too.

Energetically a woman is in the receiving role if (and only if) she is doing these things for her man through her submission to his leadership. If he directs her to do it, then she is 'receiving' the leadership and doing the act of service for him. She is letting go of control and following his lead. This is how a woman serves her man, not by anticipating his needs and desires, but by submitting to them when he (lovingly) directs her.

For a woman to follow a man's lead and it to be considered 'submission', she must be doing it without trying to get an outcome. She must do it solely because she respects her man's leadership and has faith that he is considering her. Imagine a man you deeply respect and want to follow. A man who cherishes you and gives you everything you need and more. Imagine yourself following him because it feels good to follow his lead. This is 'letting go' of control. This is submission.

It's submission when he gives you leadership to follow to meet your needs, and it's submission when he gives you leadership to follow to meet his needs.

But for it to be submission, a woman must always honor her heart when following her man's leadership. It must always be an energetic 'yes'. It should feel good and right and 'natural'.

Sometimes a woman will feel anxious when submitting, but there will also be a feeling of letting go, which requires an energy of relaxing and opening up.

If you've ever danced with a man where you felt good and could relax following his lead, this is what I'm talking about. You didn't feel like a slave when following his lead during the dance, right? You didn't feel subjugated? You didn't feel 'less than'? Good. Now apply that dynamic to all aspects of dating and in a relationship.

However, much of the time a woman is not submitting when she follows a man's lead on dates or in a relationship because she's not letting go of control. It might look like submission on the surface because she's following his lead, but she's following in an attempt to control an outcome. There are four main outcomes a woman may be trying to get when following a man's lead:

1. Getting approval – This includes trying to get the man to give her more time, compliments, affection, support and help, or physical gifts. Most women do this to get love. She is consciously or unconsciously following him so that he will love her more. Though some women do it to get 'stuff' (ie; gold diggers).

2. Avoiding disapproval – This includes trying to avoid his judgments and blame, a loss of love and/or attraction, and especially abandonment.

3. Making him happy – This is to try to 'please' her man because she wants to make him happy, make him feel respected, or make him feel 'like a man'. Obviously a healthy woman wants her man to feel good, but if she's energetically trying to make him good by following him, she's controlling.

4. Avoiding making him unhappy – This is because a woman doesn't want to hurt a man's feelings by rejecting him, so she tries to manage his feelings by doing things that hurt herself.

When a woman follows a man to get an outcome, she is controlling. The control is very subtle and is often unconscious to the woman. Often it is a childhood pattern a woman gets stuck in because she had to adjust her behavior to avoid a parent's anger or abuse, or to get their love and attention.

Following a man in this way will not feel good. A woman will not enjoy it, but she will feel like she must or 'something bad will happen' and her needs will go unmet. For many women, this pattern is so deeply engrained that they think that it's supposed to feel that way when following a man's lead.

This is not submission, this is what I call 'compliance.' There is a world of difference between compliance and submission, even if the behaviors look identical. Intent changes everything.

When a woman complies, she is always dishonoring her heart. It's always an energetic 'no'. It will feel bad, wrong, and heavy. It will feel like work and she will almost always be feeling anxious. These feelings will not necessarily feel intense, sometimes they will if she is allowing herself to be violated or if she does something that will truly hurt her. But much of the time the feeling will be very subtle, almost imperceptible.

When a woman complies, she isn't truly receiving a man. She may be doing what he wants, she may be accepting the 'gift' of his leadership, but she isn't receiving. Receiving is only possible when a woman let's go of the control. A woman can only let go of control when she is fully honoring her heart.

An extreme example of this would be complying to sex when a woman isn't 'ready' yet. Many women are unfortunately familiar with how they feel when they dishonor their hearts in this way, and they deal with the emotional repercussions afterwards. Whereas when a woman submits to sex, she is doing it when she feels ready. When she submits, she will enjoy the gift of sex, assuming the man is any good at it.

Here are some examples of compliance I experienced from women:

A woman complied when I told her to buy food for me.

A woman complied when I told her I wanted to live with her rent-free.

A woman complied when I told her to drive me around.

A woman complied (by staying in the relationship) when I told her I was going to sleep with other women.

A woman complied when I told her to take me to a resort and pay for it.

A woman complied when I told her to cook food for me (which normally isn't a problem except I rarely did anything for her to reciprocate).

A woman complied when I told her she's in charge of cleaning (which normally isn't a problem except I rarely did anything for her to reciprocate).

How would you describe this leadership? Selfish? Non-reciprocal? Inconsiderate? You probably wouldn't describe it as a 'gift', am I right?

That's because it's not a gift. Leadership is only a gift to a woman when it is considering a woman's needs and feelings. That doesn't mean a man must always be selfless and not lead a woman to meet his needs. But he should always be considering her in the big picture and he should always take serious his responsibility of being in the giving role.

Another way that women comply with undevoted leadership is by following a man when he is emotionally off-center. By off-center, I mean a man who is being judgmental, critical, blaming, yelling, or controlling. This leadership is not a gift either. When a woman complies with it, she is communicating that she deserves to be treated that way.

A woman will never feel good following leadership that is off-center. She will feel anxious, anger, shame, guilt, or some other uncomfortable feeling. Remember, submission is supposed to feel good. If you don't feel good following a man's leadership, he is probably not giving that leadership as a gift. There is likely something that is wrong.

When a woman complies with leadership that is not a gift because it's selfish or off-center, what is she getting? She's getting a burden. She's willingly taking on that burden in a conscious or unconscious effort to control and get her needs met. Which means her compliance is making the dynamic transactional, and it's a transaction that probably will not end up in her favor.

For the first few years of my marriage, my wife drove me

around everywhere. I never drove. I took the receiving role in the passenger seat. I did lead my wife to drive, which means she was following my lead, however she was following my lead to do something that should be the man's role. I wasn't considering her in that decision.

Think of driving a car in a similar way to driving a relationship. If a man told his woman to fully take charge of the relationship and the direction it is going in, is he leading? Nope. He's abdicating his role. Just because he told her to lead doesn't mean he's the leader. The same goes for driving a car.

I had a few semi-valid justifications for leading my wife to always drive: My eyesight wasn't great due to lasik gone bad. I was a significantly less experienced driver than my wife because I'd lived downtown in Toronto most of my life without a car. We also only had her car, I didn't own one and had never owned one, because public transit was easier, cheaper, and usually faster.

But none of those justifications would have been valid enough had my instincts to step into the giving role been fully online. The real reason I was in the receiving role was because I felt no motivation to be anywhere else. It didn't bother me for my wife to drive me around. It did bother her, but not as much as it should have, because her instincts were not fully online either.

When my wife followed my leadership to drive, she was dishonoring her heart. She knew she didn't enjoy it, and she knew I was being lazy and selfish. But she did it anyway because she knew I would make a fuss and be pigheaded in my beliefs and she would get nowhere. She knew me well.

My wife was complying to avoid the outcome of me getting upset and starting an argument. But for a woman to always honor her heart, she must be willing to experience consequences of being true to herself. Honoring her heart must be a non-negotiable, because if she doesn't value her heart, why would anyone else?

Luckily for us, my instincts came online after our son's birth, and everything changed very quickly. Suddenly I didn't enjoy it when my wife would drive anymore. Worse, I felt irritation when she drove. Something just felt 'off' and 'unnatural'. When instincts come online, a lot of things that seemed fine will no longer seem fine. A man won't enjoy a woman anticipating his needs, nor will he enjoy leading her to do something that he should be doing for her. There is no going back.

That was why I told my wife she isn't driving anymore. I took the drivers seat and drove everywhere. When we did our eight hour trips to visit her parents, I drove the whole way. When we were going out together, I drove. When she had an appointment or wanted to shop at the mall, I drove unless I had somewhere else I had to be. I refused to let her drive and I enjoyed taking on that responsibility to make my wife's life easier. All of a sudden I was leading while considering her needs, rather than leading selfishly. Guess what? She started to love it rather quickly.

But most women won't be lucky enough to currently have a man, or some day attract a man whose instincts are completely online. Instead, most women have men or will have men who at least some of the time lead selfishly, if they lead at all. If a woman complies rather than submits to this leadership, not only is she not in the receiving role, but she is demotivating him from truly stepping into the giving role. She demotivates him because she isn't receiving him, she's covertly controlling with her compliance.

When a woman complies, she is communicating that she has little value. So little, that she would dishonor her heart to try to get what she wants or needs from a man. Men are inspired to give when women communicate that they are valuable, and they are uninspired to give when they communicate that they lack value by complying with undevoted leadership. Complying enables the selfish or off-centered leadership, because a man can continue to get away with it.

When a woman complies, a man will sense it on some level. He will sense her lack of self worth, and he will lose attraction and inspiration to serve her. The more a woman complies, the more she demonstrates low self worth, and the lower a man's attraction and inspiration gets. If such a woman is single, she will tend to attract selfish and/or abusive men. If she's in a relationship, she will bring out the most selfish and/or abusive parts of him.

The result is that she will experience a relationship where she is receiving very little of the cherishing she needs. Her man will not be in the giving role consistently, because he will energetically be doing a lot of taking. But guess what? Because the woman is trying to control through complying, she's also trying to take, but in a more subtle way.

Complying turns a relationship into a take-take dynamic. Whereas receiving turns a relationship into a receive-give dynamic. These two dynamics can look very similar on the surface, but they couldn't be more different energetically.

We will go back to Fred and Wilma to understand why this is. Imagine if Wilma was willing to sexually submit to Fred to get pregnant, without any indication that he would provide for her. She gets pregnant, and he goes off to have sex with other cave-ladies and to play cave people-videogames all day. This is a cave-lady's (and woman's) worst nightmare. If it were to happen, the survival of her genes would be in serious jeopardy. Her instincts would warn her by making her feel extremely anxious.

However, she continues to submit to him sexually. She submits because she hopes that if she gives Fred what he wants, he will eventually see her as worthy of providing for. But it never works. Fred realizes he can get away with not providing for Wilma and Wilma will still receive him sexually. When this happens, another instinctual program kicks in. I call it the 'man whore' program:

Fred's genes know that the best chance of replication is to continue having sex with Wilma (since she's allowing it), while also going off to find another cave-woman to have sex with and provide for. His sperm regenerates daily, so there is very low genetic cost and potential big genetic reward for doing this.

Fred's genes will be programmed to lose inspiration to provide for Wilma when she complies to his undevoted leadership by submitting to him sexually without him providing resources. He will also experience a huge drop of attraction. The drop of attraction won't be big enough to lose all desire to have sex with Wilma (because it makes genetic sense to continue doing so), but it will be enough of a drop that he is motivated to find more women to procreate with. This won't be a logical decision that Fred reasoned out, his emotions are compelling him into this behavior.

From a purely genetic survival standpoint, Fred is being very smart. His genetic offspring with Wilma might survive (it's a gamble) but even if they don't, he will still be providing for another woman who is having children with him. Those offspring will be more likely to survive.

But from a genetic survival standpoint, Wilma is being very

dumb. Such a strategy will eventually result in her genetic line probably dying out.

Which is why a cave-lady's instincts are programmed to compel her to never engage in such a mating strategy.

But modern women engage in this strategy often, submitting (complying) to sex and submitting (complying) to leadership even when the man is not Devoted to taking care of her. The reason women do this is because unlike cave-ladies, women today often have childhood wounding that compels them into behaviors that go against their instincts. Even though a woman's instincts tell her that she shouldn't comply to undevoted leadership, she does it anyway in an unconscious attempt to get what she wants, or avoid what she doesn't want.

A woman complying with a man's undevoted leadership doesn't necessarily mean he will go into manwhore mode and cheat on her. Many men do have morals and willpower and won't cheat no matter how little self worth a woman demonstrates that she has. But the more she complies to undevoted leadership, the less attracted and inspired he will be. Complying to undevoted leadership will only result in even more undevoted leadership.

A woman's body is always telling her when she should submit to a man's leadership, if she is in tune with it. Her body knows when something is off. It knows when she is being subjugated. It knows when she isn't being considered. Sometimes what she is feeling is due to wounding, which makes it more complicated to read her instinctual body signals, but underneath that is always her instinct which is telling her the truth.

If a woman has self worth issues, she will be very inclined to follow leadership when it isn't serving her. She will comply to leadership that is giving her breadcrumbs and even abuse. Even though she doesn't feel good complying, she believes she would feel even worse by not getting the love she craves, or by being abandoned.

To make things even more difficult for the woman, she will likely be justifying her behavior in her mind to avoid facing the truth of what she's doing to herself. Have you ever told yourself anything like the following:

"He doesn't mean to be like this."

"He's just having a bad day."

"Once he knows how much I love him he will treat me better."

"It could be a lot worse."

"I just want to be helpful."

"I deserve this."

The first step to shifting this compliance pattern is to see what you are doing, and to see the rationalizations you make to justify the behavior. Once you see the truth and stop lying to yourself, it gets a lot easier.

The next step is knowing what to do when a man leads you to do something that would be dishonoring your heart. This creates a tricky problem, and the answer to solve it is one of the most sought out answers by all women throughout time.

My wife tried to tell me many times that she didn't enjoy the role she was in and told me to drive, and I told her no. I wasn't purposely trying to be selfish or hurt her, I just had a different (and unhealthy) perspective than she did about why she should drive. I became increasingly resistant to change my perspective because she was leading me to do so instead of communicating her feelings and needs with respect. Eventually she stopped trying. She knew it was a recipe for failure. Many women reading this will likely relate.

Feminine communication fixes this.

"May I share a feeling?"

"Yes."

"I feel a lot of frustration and anger."

"Oh. Why?"

"Because when I drive you around, I feel like your mother. I miss feeling like your wife."

Notice how the woman in the example is angry, but she doesn't blame or judge the man. She focuses on her feelings and how the problem is impacting her. Also notice that she doesn't give the man a solution or set a boundary. That would just be hopping out of the frying pan into the fire, from complying to leading. Instead, she acts on faith that her man will come up with a solution, hopefully realizing that he needs to be the man and get himself into the giving role.

Feminine communication is how a woman can extricate herself from complying. She must let go of control so she can shift from taking into receiving. But because she is in control patterns due to fear, that fear will make it very difficult to let go of the control. She has been complying her entire life in a desperate attempt to get her needs met and to not be abandoned. It's easier said than done to let that all go and risk the perceived consequences. It will take an enormous amount of courage. That's why she can and should also have conversations with her man about her compliance control patterns.

"May I share my feelings?"

"Sure."

"I feel fear."

"Oh, why?"

"Because I'm afraid you'll abandon me if I don't continue driving you around."

"Oh. I had no idea. You don't want to drive me around?"

"No, I feel anger and exhaustion when I do. I start to feel like a man."

"Oh, I didn't realize it bothered you so much. I'll start driving then."

Notice again that there is no blame or judgment here in the words. A woman must ensure that there is none. If there is blame or judgment, it will only entrench a man further into his position, or it will shift him into doing what she wants out of obligation and he will only continue doing it out of willpower rather than Devotion. Her communication must be vulnerable and respectful. This is what a man needs to experience for him to be inspired to relieve you of this burden that he imposed on you.

Either of these options are what I would have needed from my wife if my instinct didn't come online on its own. Her communicating in this way would have started to activate that instinct because it is so respectful and feminine. I would be inspired to relieve her from the burden as a gift to her, which would cause me to feel good because it's through my leadership.

As soon as a woman speaks up for her needs by permissively and vulnerably using feminine communication, guess what happens? She steps out of the compliance-based control pattern. She stops taking, and opens herself up to receive. In this moment, she is giving a man respect, while simultaneously honoring her own feelings and needs. She's opening herself to receive his leadership and solution to the problem. This tends to inspire devotion in a man, and compels him into the giving role to adjust his leadership or give her direction or reassurance.

Magic.

However, the magic will not work 100% of the time, with 100% of men, even if her energy is pure. If it doesn't work, she needs to be willing to not comply with what her man told her to do. It's OK for a woman to not follow a man's lead when he is not considering her. That's not disrespectful, he is already disrespecting himself by lacking consideration. But she should still express herself in a feminine way, to give respect. Even when a man isn't being respectable.

"May I share a problem?"

"Sure."

"I can't do what you want."

"Why not?"

"Because I'd be dishonoring my heart to submit and I will feel bad if I do it. May I have some help?"

This is not setting a boundary. Setting a boundary (by my definition) is creating a wall and making it clear to the other partner not to cross it.

"Don't tell me what to do."

Or

"Don't lead me without considering my needs."

Those are boundaries. That is directive masculine energy. It is based on control. A woman can't set boundaries and tell a man that she's not doing what he says anymore if she wants to inspire him. If her man respected the boundary, it wouldn't be done out of inspiration, it would be done out of obligation, because she's leading. He would be doing what she wants, but through him complying, rather than leading. There would be no love given, and the woman will not feel cherished.

Instead, the woman is expressing a problem that she has. She is energetically remaining open and receptive to provision. She is in the receiving role when she does this. It's not a boundary. It's a problem she's asking for help with. She is asking for her man's gift of leadership. That is feminine communication.

Her permissive question asking for help compels him into the giving role to give her a gift. That gift is a solution to the problem she presented. Depending on the reason she is struggling to submit, that gift might be reassurance, clarity, or adjusting his leadership with what he wants her to do.

... Unless of course, a man is unwilling to adjust his leadership to help his woman truly submit, rather than comply. Even when she stays feminine and continues to use feminine communication to explain the problem. What a man is demonstrating from this lack of interest is that he does not care about his woman's feelings and needs. He is not willing to step into the giving role because he would prefer to remain a taker.

It is at this point that a woman needs to question whether to stay with that man. She can't comply, because she'd be dishonoring her heart. She doesn't want to resist, because then she is in her masculine to energetically protect herself from her man. So she will have to leave.

Not necessarily right away.

If it's a first date, there is little investment and such leadership from a man is such a massive red flag that a woman is likely wasting her time if she sticks around.

Whereas if she's married with children, there's enormous investment, and it will likely be worth it to have a lot more of these conversations (and ideally be coached on the nuance of doing so), staying in her feminine energy. But for as long as she stays, she shouldn't comply.

Women with feminine self worth only submit.

CHAPTER 8

HOW TO STOP LEADING

The fourth way that women fail to stay in the receiving role is by leading a man. Often, ironically, in a futile attempt to try to get him to step up into the giving role. 'Leading him to lead.'

When I usually refer to the term 'lead' I am referring to the energy of trying to get an outcome. Which technically a woman is always doing if she's not in the receiving role. But for this chapter I am going to narrow down my meaning of leading to when a woman is 'in charge', energetically. Not necessarily all of the time or in every area of the relationship, but at least some of the time and in at least one area of the relationship.

At the extreme (where a woman is in charge all of the time) here is how this dynamic can look:

1. She is in charge overtly, she's very clearly the one that 'wears the pants'. She gives her man directives and judgments about his behavior.

2. She is in charge covertly and it may not be obvious that she wears the pants because she may seem like the feminine one in the relationship. She is soft, but she's still trying to get outcomes.

A man will lose motivation to be in the giving role when a woman is energetically leading the relationship and has all the power, or is co-leading the relationship and 'sharing' power, or is leading aspects of the relationship some of the time and has some of the power. If she has all of the power, she will feel like his mother. If she shares power with him, she will feel like a roommate. If she holds on to some of the power, she may feel like his woman but he will be less inspired to serve her than he should. Men only feel inspired to be in the giving role all of the time when their woman is not in charge in the relationship and is in the receiving role all of the time.

Women often believe that they need to have power in the relationship to be respected and considered. But this is not true. They do need to honor their hearts by not complying with undevoted leadership if they want a Devoted man. But they do not need power and control.

Consider this; do fathers naturally want to cherish their five-year old daughters? Reflect on the healthy fathers you know of and how they treat their daughters with love and want to give them the world.

The daughter doesn't have any 'power'. The daughter is not 'in charge'. She is submitting to the fathers lead and respecting his decisions (as much as a five year old can). He feels devotion not despite having all the power, but because he has all the power. He is compelled into the giving role to use that power to serve his daughter, it's natural.

For example, my daughter is (at the time of this book release) one and a half years old. She has no power with me. In fact, she is completely helpless and I could do whatever I want to her. What do I choose to do with that power? I choose to love her with it. I choose to make sure all of her needs are met, and many of her desires are met. I choose to give her kisses and hugs until she squeals with delight. I choose to entertain her when she's playful, and console her when she's sad. The idea of doing anything to hurt her or take advantage of her in any way never enters my head, because all I am interested in doing is making her life better.

Now, there are a couple of issues with this comparison.

Firstly, some fathers are not healthy and do not treat their daughters with love. But I'm not talking about those men. Those men should be avoided for a relationship.

Secondly, my daughter has half of my genes. My instincts are going to naturally compel me to give to my daughter because she has my genes, whereas my wife does not.

Thirdly, women are not children.

But what this comparison does is illustrate how sharing power is not necessarily required to be treated well. My experience in my marriage further cements this assertion.

In my marriage, I have all of the power, my wife has none. I make all of the decisions, I tell her what I want her to do and what I expect, she doesn't set boundaries with me or lead me to do anything. She uses feminine communication to share her problems and feelings, and to ask me permission for what she wants or needs. I treat her well and I take my job seriously to make her happy and not cause her harm with the power I have.

When she tries to lead (which she does at times accidentally) I start to lose devotion to serve her, though I lead her into letting go of that control to re-establish my devotion.

When she doesn't lead and communicates with respect as the 'follower', I feel devotion to serve her.

The reason why a man feels less devotion the more power and control a woman has in the relationship is because respect fuels his devotion. The more respect a woman communicates to him, the more devotion he feels. When she doesn't lead him, she communicates that she trusts him and respects him as her leader. When she tries to control him, she is communicating that she doesn't trust or respect him as the leader.

When a man's instincts are at least partially online, he will feel irritation whenever a woman tries to lead and control him. This irritation is warning him that something is wrong. The more she leads, the more irritated he will become, and the less Devotion he will have in his heart. If you have a man or have experienced a man who gets easily irritated and resistant, there is a good chance that you are seeing his masculine instinct at work. It is compelling him into not energetically complying to your control.

Many women see this as a bad thing. They believe that men who get easily irritated with them are wounded. Granted, some of that irritation likely is wounding. If he's not centering himself and leading you with love out of trying to control, there is certainly some wounding. But at the root, that irritation is his instincts telling him that there is something wrong. Unfortunately, men typically don't know what to do with that irritation and tend to take it out on women in unhealthy ways. I'm not justifying that, but I am pointing out how that irritation tends to be a sign that a woman is energetically trying to control, and that the irritation itself is a good thing.

Before my masculine instincts came fully online, I always felt this irritation when my wife tried to lead and control. Whenever she stepped into that energy, I never wanted to do anything for her. I was far more selfish back then, and not devoted, but her trying to lead brought out the most stingy, lazy, and self-interested parts of me. I would almost always go into resistance, or I would get upset and argue with her. I was energetically much more in charge of the relationship than she was overall. But she held onto enough power that my instincts to Devote to her were not activated.

When my instincts fully came online, I wanted to give more to my wife. I wanted to 'take care' of her and be responsible for taking care of her. I wanted to make her life easier with all the work she was doing by taking care of our son. Unfortunately, she tried to lead me to take care of her and make her life easier, because she didn't know any other way to communicate. She'd almost be demanding when leading me to get diapers and clean bottles and make sure that lights were on and off.

This behavior caused me even more irritation than before my instincts came online. The reason was because I was at a point where I needed to be in the giving role, I needed to take care of her, I needed to be her Devotional man. I felt that strong desire to devote to her, and to have her respect. But because she continued to try to control me, I received a lot of disrespect instead. Prior to my instincts coming online, I didn't see it as a necessity to respect me by never leading me in any way. I found it irritating when she led me, but I could shake it off easily. However, when my instincts came online I needed to be respected for being in the giving role, and so the irritation was much stronger. The instinct brings the need for total respect online, and with it, irritation when that need is not met.

It wasn't only irritation that I experienced. I also felt sadness. I felt sad because I felt that strong desire to lead my wife with care. To be in that respected position of authority with her. To be able to cherish her like I could so effortlessly cherish my son. Her trying to lead me to the extent that she did made it impossible for me to give her the love she needed, because a man can't give a woman love when she is leading him to meet her needs. He can give her kisses and clean up bottles and make plans and all of that stuff. He can 'go through the motions'. But he will not be doing any of it out of Devotion, it will be done out of obligation because his woman is leading him to do it.

If a woman finds a man with his instincts relatively online, her control will only ever result in resistance and irritation from him. These relationships tend to have a lot of conflict and arguments, and both man and woman aren't happy. If you've experienced this with a man, that's almost certainly why.

But there are many relationships where it looks like the man is in charge superficially. He is technically making the big decisions and it looks like he's the 'leader'. He plans the dates and trips and might be the financial provider. He buys his woman gifts and chocolates and does all kinds of nice stuff. In many ways he looks like a great example of what I describe a man should be.

But in reality, he's covertly complying to his woman and her energy. She's covertly leading the relationship, and often quite unintentionally. To grasp what I'm trying to describe here, think of the typical nice guy 'beta' male. He does all the 'right' things and may look perfect on paper, but women don't want him. A woman might eventually settle for him because he can provide and take care of her (at least on a superficial level), but he doesn't turn her on. He doesn't command her respect.

We are going to go back to the cave people yet again to make sense of this dynamic.

Let's say that Fred is a little scrawny runt, half the size of any other cave-man. He sees Wilma walking through the forest and thinks she's gorgeous. But he knows he isn't worthy enough for her because of his size. He doesn't think he 'has what it takes' to get with a cave-lady that fine. So what does he do? He gets a bunch of food and brings it back to her to impress her in the hopes that she will sexually submit to him and his genes carried in his sperm.

What he is communicating through this act is that he doesn't believe he has high quality genes. He is communicating that by having his children, Wilma will lower the survival chances of her genes. He is communicating that he needs a whole bunch of food to make up for the low value of his sperm and the burden that he would be placing on her by mixing her genes with his and being stuck raising his child.

A high-value caveman who knows his worth does not believe he needs to do or give anything to get a woman to sexually submit. He knows subconsciously that his sex, his sperm, his genes, his penis is the gift. He subconsciously knows that having sex with a woman will increase her chance of gene survival because his genes have so much value. He provides and protects a cave-lady because he wants to increase her value and make her feel special. It's all about her, not his self-worth deficiency. That's the kind of cave-man that every cave-woman is wired to be attracted to and submit to. That's the kind of cave-man that Wilma wants.

Wilma would consider Fred in this dynamic if there were no better options because the cave-men with the amazing genes were all paired off with other females and providing for them. In such a predicament, her instincts compel her into a new genetic survival strategy. She can't have the provision from a cave-man with high genetic value that she wants. But she can accept the resources from the runty provider, and (in secret) sexually submit to a cave-man that has much higher quality genes. She will be compelled into this behavior by still feeling desire to receive resources from Fred the runt, but with little to no attraction for him. Fred the runt feels like 'just a friend'. Her levels of attraction are her instincts telling her whether her genes are likely to survive by mating.

While she has little attraction for runty Fred, she does have lots of attraction for Johnny the cave-man next door. She will take his sperm, while letting Fred provide resources to her. Fred is willing to continuing providing resources to her in the hope that some day she will sexually submit to him and his genes.

Understand that the drop of attraction that Wilma experiences isn't caused by Fred being a runt, that may be a tiny factor at most. The main factor is Fred's perception of his own value to a woman. His perception that he is of little value causes a huge drop in self confidence which compels him into the low value behavior of giving to get. When he does this, he abdicates his power in the relationship and Wilma is in control. When she senses that she has the power and that Fred perceives that he lacks genetic survival value, attraction goes out the window. This is all instinctual programming to maximize her genetic survival chances.

This is exactly what happens with many modern relationships today. Women settle for a man because he can be in the provider role, even if she isn't very attracted to him due to his lack of power. Or a woman is initially attracted to him because he was good at acting the part of a man with value, but the costume comes off later in the relationship and she ends up with the power.

Such a man seems to be in the giving role in what he does, but he isn't in the giving role energetically. He's not cherishing, he's making up for his self-perceived value deficiency. It's obligatory giving. Giving to get. Giving to be 'good enough' for the woman to sexually submit. Not giving to give love. This is rarely conscious. If you ask such a man what he's doing, few will have any level of awareness, but this is what is driving his behavior. Which is why their woman lacks attraction and interest in sex.

That doesn't mean every single woman in such a dynamic is going to cheat on her man with Johnny next door. Many women have a sense of morals and some level willpower. But what matters is that the more power she has in the relationship, the more her body wants her to cheat. Her instincts will try to compel her into cheating because she will have a low level of attraction and respect for her man and a huge spike of attraction for a man who she can sense has the power that her man lacks.

A woman in such a position will not feel cherished by her man, even if he gives and gives and gives. To be cherished, a man must be giving his woman love from a position of strength, power, leadership, and control. He's doing it because he's in charge in the relationship, and he's using his power to serve his woman. When he does this, a woman feels amazing. She melts. Her instincts are telling her that this is exactly the dynamic she needs for her genes to thrive. She feels special, protected, cared for. Cherished.

But when a man plays the giving role 'part' when the woman has much or all of the power, he's in that role for the wrong reasons. He's doing it either because he believes that's what a man is 'supposed' to do (complying to societies expectations). Or he's doing it for approval or to avoid disapproval (complying with his woman's leadership). Either way, it's due to a lack of masculine self worth. For this reason, it will usually be obligatory. His woman won't melt. She won't feel much attraction. She might even feel like his mother or his roommate.

If a man's instincts are offline he might enjoy or not mind the inverted dynamic where he covertly complies. Whereas if his instincts are online, a man will loath every moment of covertly complying but may go through the motions to get what he wants if he doesn't believe he is worthy of his woman's respect. But if a man's instincts are online and he believes he is worthy of his woman's respect, he won't be able to tolerate complying to his woman for long. This was the situation I found myself in with my wife.

I did try ignoring my irritation for a while when I was helping my wife with our son. I ignored the irritation because I felt so much Devotion for my son that I was willing to feel terrible if it meant him getting the support he needed from my wife and I. But it was almost unbearable. I felt increasingly angry towards my wife and even with my background in meditation and self help, the negative feelings continued to get worse instead of better. My instincts simply would not allow me to continue complying, because I knew subconsciously that I deserved respect. I did not have a self worth problem, and I wanted to Devote. But I couldn't do that when my wife was trying to control me, because her control caused me to lose inspiration to Devote to her.

As with all dynamics between a man and a woman, the man has a ton of responsibility for creating this situation. That should be obvious to anyone. He should learn to take back the power in his relationship by leading his woman out of controlling behavior by teaching her to let go and use feminine communication. He should also learn to stop complying with any controlling behavior she exhibits. That's how my marriage ended up changing.

But what many women may not realize is that women also have a ton of responsibility for creating this unpleasant situation too. This kind of behavior occurs when a man can sense a woman's power (masculine energy), and he is attracted to it because his own is not fully online. The more powerful a woman, the more she will attract weak men. Also, the more powerful a woman, the more a weak man will covertly submit to her power and lead.

A woman can fix these issues by fixing herself. She fixes herself by completely letting go of all power and control, either when dating or in a relationship. If a woman is in tune with her body, she will feel it when she is energetically leading. She will also be in tune to when a man is complying, even when he's playing the part doing all the 'right' things looking like a provider and protector. When this dynamic happens, she must use feminine communication.

"May I share what I am feeling?"

"Sure."

"I feel disgust."

"Oh why?"

"Because I can feel I'm in control in the relationship and I don't want to have any control. But I also keep doing things to stay in control. May I have help?"

In this moment, the woman has used feminine communication to shift herself into the receiving role. The more that she uses feminine communication to ask for help when she notices she's controlling or notices her man complying, the more that she inspires her man to step up and take control back. She also inspires him to find a way to help her let go of that control.

But control is sneaky, especially when a woman lacks enough

self awareness. It can be so sneaky that a woman could master feminine communication and still be stuck in control. You could take all of the information I've given you about feminine communication in this book and use it to stay in control. The control would be more subtle than it was before because it looks like you are being feminine superficially, but nothing fundamental has changed. You'd be just as controlling, but with a femininity costume to hide it better.

Feminine communication can help a woman shift her energy to let go of control when its used for that purpose.

But it can also be used to help a woman become better at getting what she wants while holding tight onto control.

This is the danger. When feminine communication is used to energetically let go of control, a woman heals. She opens up into her femininity, heals all the pain in her heart, and inspires a man into devotion.

But when feminine communication is used to control a man, a woman doesn't heal. The woman creates a femininity costume, and co-creates a dynamic with a man where it looks like he is leading and she is submitting. But in truth, he is covertly complying to the control, and she is covertly leading using a very effective language.

This could never work with a man when his instincts are fully online, his instincts will sense the manipulation and he will feel irritation whenever she communicates.

But it can work very well on a man if his instincts are not online.

I know many men and women relationship coaches who teach

some of the same things I teach, but their relationships are completely inverted in this way. The woman is in control. They are acting out something that looks like traditional gender roles, but none of it is real. She may not know it. He may not know it either. Their clients don't know it. But that is what is happening. They are putting on a play that they do not realize they are acting in.

A man can never be inspired into devotion when the woman is in control, even if her control is very covert and almost imperceptible. He can only ever be compelled into compliance. A man may not be consciously aware of what is happening, but his suppressed instincts will know.

A man is only inspired into Devotionally giving from the giving role when he has the control and his woman does not. Only when his woman is giving him true respect and trust by letting go of control will he feel Devotion and act on it. There is no other way. There is no shortcut. There is no acting job good enough to make it happen. It must be real.

The challenge here is that letting go of control is terrifying for women who are used to being in control, and who stay in control in an effort to 'stay safe' and 'not get hurt'. Becoming feminine isn't as simple as learning a new language. That's easy. Becoming feminine is more like climbing up a cliff and your harness is attached to a man, and the man is free climbing with no safety equipment. If you fall, you must have faith that he will be strong enough to hold on so he can bring you back up. You also must have faith that he doesn't fall first.

It's in letting go of control that the real work starts for a woman. The work has not even begun until then. She must let go of the overt control, and she must let go of the sneaky covert control. Pay attention to how you feel in your body when communicating and interacting with a man. Your body is your guide here.

When you are controlling, you will feel tight, tense, anxious, and rigid. When you are letting go of control you will feel light, free, juicy, and open.

Your body will tell you whether you are controlling. Focus on letting go, and focus on asking for help letting go if you are struggling.

CHAPTER 9

HOW TO RECEIVE WITH GRATITUDE

The fifth and final way that women fail to stay in the receiving role is by not feeling and / or showing gratitude when receiving a man's gift.

Here are a few ways various women have not been unable to feel or show gratitude at certain times with me:

When I had given a woman a compliment.

When I had driven a woman to the mall.

When I had put an effort into cleaning the house / apartment for a woman.

When I had planned a fun date for a woman.

When I had planned a fun trip for a woman.

When I had given a woman advice.

When I was single, I met a lot of women. When I say 'a lot', I mean thousands and thousands, if not tens of thousands. I met most women in stores, coffee shops, bars, clubs, or even on the sidewalk. I would go up to them and start a conversation. I would usually initiate the conversation with a woman by telling her that I thought she was beautiful (or some other synonym about her looks). When I gave that compliment, I meant it. It wasn't a tactic to get her to like me, it was my authentic truth in that moment and it came from a place of power. Women felt it.

What happened next with each woman was very illustrative of the importance of feeling and expressing gratitude to inspire a man's Devotion.

Some women I complimented didn't seem positively effected one bit. They acted as if they didn't care that they got such a nice compliment, and that a man had taken time to let her know what he thought of her.

Others seemed to have a mildly positive response. They smiled, they were receptive, they said *"thanks"*.

Some complimented me back.

Finally, some women responded wildly positively. Communicating that I had made their day. They were clearly happy, all smiles, fully open. The best way I can describe it is how a five year old girl would respond when she gets her dream barbie house on Christmas day.

Now it's time to put on your thinking caps. Which women do you think activated my masculine instincts to want to stay in the giving role and give even more attention, time, energy, and compliments?

Right. The ones who received me, fully, with gratitude and joy. The ones where my gift had a strong noticeable positive effect. When a woman demonstrates clear gratitude for a gift, a man feels compelled to give her more because he feels received.

Whereas the ones who didn't respond positively or responded with only mild positivity did not create this effect. You could say it was because they just didn't like me or they didn't like me very much. Fair enough. Not every woman likes me, is attracted to me, or enjoys my very strong and direct approach. So for at least some of these women, that was true.

However, I know that was not the case for all of those women. Because I was persistent, I didn't give up when a woman gave me a less than ideal response. I would stay and continue to talk to them, and help them become comfortable. This wasn't coming from genuine desire, because my interest in them would plummet immediately if they did not respond well to my gift. It came from willpower and a determination to be as confident and unshakeable as I could possibly be and not let a woman's reactions, mood, or reception stop me.

Here's what I discovered from talking to these women:

Many of the women who responded poorly initially were attracted to me from the start. But they had a problem: They either didn't believe that they were worthy of my gift and thus felt shame instead of gratitude, or they didn't know what to do in that situation and felt anxious instead of gratitude, or they tried to 'play it cool' so that they didn't indicate that they were 'too interested'. In all cases, they didn't fully receive me, and thus they didn't express their gratitude for my gift.

One of the most extreme examples was a woman who made no indication that she enjoyed my compliment, or the ten minute conversation I had with her after it. I did 90% of the talking, and I found it extraordinarily difficult to get her talking. Throughout the entire conversation, I thought she didn't like me. I only continued the conversation and (successfully) got her number to push my comfort zone. Turns out, she liked me so much that she invited me to a party the next day by text, and when I arrived she followed me around talking to me most of the evening. She turned out to be an amazing, fun, feminine woman.

Had I acted on what I was initially feeling, I never would have asked for her number and I would have excused myself from the conversation 30 seconds after starting it. The only reason it turned out the way it did was my obsession with pushing myself through as much discomfort and anxiety as possible. I otherwise had no natural desire to continue giving her my time, energy, and attention, or leading the interaction further.

Here is the big take-away; gratitude fuels devotion. When a woman fully receives a man and his gifts, she will feel gratitude and effortlessly express that gratitude which will inspire him to give more. A lack of gratitude causes a man to lose the motivation to continue giving. Unless he is doing it from willpower, he will lose interest in giving his gifts and will focus his time and attention elsewhere (which may include focusing on other women).

If a man is truly energetically giving, he isn't giving a gift to receive gratitude back. That would be giving to get, and that isn't a gift. If I was giving compliments so women could validate me with their gratitude, all I would be doing is manipulating them. They would also be able to sense my inauthenticity on some level, and then be less likely to feel or genuinely express gratitude. Gratitude is only felt when the woman senses the gift is real and has no strings attached.

Healthy men love to give for the sake of giving, without any strings attached. They aren't trying to get anything from a woman. But, if she isn't grateful, a man will see his giving as pointless and not want to do it anymore. Would you use your money to buy presents for people who didn't appreciate them? No of course you wouldn't (unless you did it out of obligation). Nobody wants to do things for people if they don't seem to want what they are being given. They want to give to those who value what is given.

Let's use a simple example of what expressing gratitude can look like: The simple 'thankyou'. When a woman truly receives a man's gift, her simple 'thankyou' will make his day. He will feel how much his gift positively impacted her and how grateful she is to receive it. He will see her genuine smile and twinkle of her eyes. He will hear the enthusiasm in her voice. That could be all she says, and that thankyou is more than enough for him to want to give more.

But that same thankyou is meaningless if it obligatory. Think of how you have said thankyou because it's a social custom, like at the grocery store when the cashier hands you the receipt. Are you grateful? Probably not. You already have a built-in expectation and the cashier is 'just doing their job'. They met the minimum standard you expect from them, and so they get an obligatory 'thankyou'. That obligatory thankyou is not inspiring in any way, because it isn't real gratitude.

There isn't much point in going back to our cave-people friends to explain this. A woman expressing a lack of gratitude for a man's gifts has a similar but less pronounced effect on a man as a woman who resists his gifts. Resistance is when a woman is not receiving a man's gifts, and is showing displeasure or even fighting to not receive them. Whereas a lack of gratitude is when a woman does receive the gift itself, without it emotionally affecting her (or not showing that it does). The gift was received, but it wasn't received deeply. It didn't penetrate her fully.

As a sexual analogy, only 'the tip' went in. He didn't fill her fully with his penis. His whole penis wasn't received. How much fun is that for the woman or man? Not very. The real fun happens for man and woman when the woman fully receives the man's penis. Think about this analogy when you are having fun learning how to feel and show gratitude for a man's other gifts.

Now you might be thinking 'I don't have this problem, I'm very grateful. I just light up when a man gives me a compliment or a box of chocolates."

That is fantastic if that is the case. You're ahead of the game. But what about other gifts?

Do you also light up when a man gives you advice about your health or finances?

Do you also light up when he tells you (lovingly) how to be more respectful to him?

Do you also light up when he sets boundaries on how much you can spend on something?

Boundaries, advice, and direction are all gifts too, and they are very important gifts. A man who is doing his job properly in the giving role should be giving gifts like this to his woman. Are you able to receive them fully and feel gratitude for them? Or is something blocking you?

If you can't receive these gifts, not only will he start to lose interest in giving you those gifts, he will also start losing interest in giving you the gifts you are grateful for.

This gets further complicated when a man gives such gifts but not to a high degree of competence.

What if a man gives you bad advice?

What if how he wants you to be respectful doesn't make sense to you?

What if the budget he wants you to follow seems too low?

What if he got you chocolates but they are the wrong kind with the weird fake strawberry flavor that you hate and he didn't know?

Can you still be grateful? You could, if you were putting importance on a man's effort, rather than the specific result. Ask yourself if you feel gratitude when a man puts in the effort to give you something, but it wasn't what you were hoping for. Ask yourself if his love and intention is enough for you to deeply receive him. If not, there is still work to do.

Women who inspire men effortlessly would still be grateful in these situations and they would express it. But that doesn't mean that they wouldn't also be honest and use feminine communication to share the problem.

"Thankyou so much for your time helping me with this and giving me advice. May I share a problem though?"

"Yes."

"I tried that diet and I felt horrible, I gained the weight back as soon as I stopped."

See how the woman in this situation is fully receiving the man's gift, even though the gift wasn't helpful? That's because she has learned how to receive his love driving the gift, rather than focusing on the gift itself. Having this very rare ability will result in an amazing outcome: Even if the man was not very good at being competent in giving certain gifts at first, he would be inspired to get better, for her. He would be inspired because he would feel her gratitude, and want to experience more of it.

From reading this example, you might be thinking that I am advocating being fake and inauthentic, because you couldn't imagine feeling such gratitude for real in certain situations.

But I am not advocating that. Gratitude cannot be faked. Even if a woman is a superb actress, a man's instincts know the difference between fake gratitude and real gratitude. If it's fake, he will not feel received and thus will not feel inspired to give more. Worse, the woman would have to dishonor herself to put on such an act, and a woman should never do that.

A woman is likely to fake gratitude when she is stuck trying to control outcomes. She may try to be grateful to not hurt her man's feelings, or to make him happy, or to get more of what she wants. I've had many women try to fake some level of gratitude when I would meet them or date them, and it is usually obvious, and uninspiring.

For a man to be inspired to continue giving, the gratitude must be real. It must be truly felt, and it must be expressed because a woman can't help but express it. This is not about trying to get a man to be in the giving role. You can't get him there strategically, through manipulation. The best you can ever achieve by acting is to get him also acting the part of being in the giving role when really he is covertly complying to your subtle control.

For the gratitude to be real, you need to stop trying to do anything. You must express simply because you feel gratitude, and can't help but share it.

When you were a little kid, did you ever receive something that just made you so happy that you couldn't contain yourself? Maybe you were taken to the zoo, or maybe your dad bought you your favorite ice-cream. When you shared your pleasure, it wasn't to try to make your dad happy. It was because the pleasure was so pleasurable, it just had to be expressed. It had to come out.

Right now I'm thinking about my one and a half year old daughter. I smile at her or play 'peek a boo' with her or give her a big dramatic cheek kiss to make her laugh. In those moments, she's receiving me with joy. She's not trying to fake anything. She's not thinking about making sure I feel happy so I stay in the giving role. She's just receiving me with joy. That's how it must be for a man to want to continue giving. If my daughter was unresponsive to me when I try to get a positive reaction from her, I'd start to lose the joy of giving quite quickly.

For many women, expressing gratitude was much easier when they were five, than when they are thirty-five or forty-five. Between then and early to mid adulthood a woman tends to become increasingly hardened and guarded, which makes it more difficult to feel and/or express gratitude. Healing that wounding will come from being honest and letting go of control, rather than a 'fake it til you make it' approach which cannot get you what you want and need.

Women don't express gratitude for three main reasons. They don't feel worthy of the gift, they feel entitled to more, or the feel too inhibited to verbally, physically, and energetically express their gratitude.

Let's talk about each problem and as we do, I will offer an example of a viable solution for each using feminine communication.

1. Feeling unworthy of the gift.

When a woman doesn't see her value, she will not feel gratitude when she receives gifts that she perceives are 'too good' for her. Instead, she will feel shame for not being good enough to deserve it, guilt for not doing enough to deserve it, or fear of the possibility that her man will realize she is not worthy and stop giving and possibility abandon her. There's not much room to feel gratitude when experiencing these unpleasant feelings.

"May I share what I am feeling?"

"Yes."

"I feel shame."

"What? Why?"

"Because I'm telling myself a story that I don't deserve this much love and care."

This will not be as inspiring to a man as unbridled gratitude. But believe it or not, it is a second best option that will tend to elicit more love and care if the woman is expressing vulnerably from the heart. If you don't feel gratitude, you won't be able to fake it, but this way the man will know exactly what is going on. He will know that the issue is not him or his gift. He will understand that you have a wounding and he will want to help support you in working through it. Even though you were unable to receive his gift, you opened into the receiving role by being vulnerable and creating an opening for the man to serve you and help you with the problem.

2. Feeling entitled

When a woman has expectations of how things 'should' be and what she 'should' be receiving, she will be blocking herself from being able to receive. She will only rarely be able to feel gratitude, and only if a man exceeds the expectations she has for him and his gifts. A classic case is a woman who has expectations of the perfect date, so she can never appreciate a date if it rains or if the steak is slightly overcooked or if the man picks a restaurant that is not her favorite. Nothing is ever good enough for her.

"May I share a problem?"

"Yes."

"I think I'm struggling with some entitlement issues and I don't know how to feel grateful for this gift. May I have help?"

Similar to communicating when she is experiencing shame (or guilt) for believing she doesn't deserve the gift, the above communication is an example of the best option available for a woman who believes she's entitled to more. She won't be able to fake gratitude, and if she says nothing, her man will think his gifts are not good enough. Whereas sharing the problem she is experiencing creates an opening for him to give provision. In that moment, she is stepping into the receiving role and inspiring him into the giving role.

This is different than a woman who lacks self worth and accepts crumbs. If a man truly isn't putting in love and care, a woman will not feel gratitude, and she shouldn't, because she isn't being valued. Her instincts are telling her that she isn't being considered and she shouldn't downplay, ignore, or gaslight those feelings. That is very different from a woman who believes she is owed something from the world and from a man.

3. Feeling inhibited

Many women are afraid of showing their positive feelings. They are afraid of seeming too childish, or too emotional or 'too much'. They judge themselves for acting 'like a kid'. They may also worry that a man will settle for giving her crumbs if she shows gratitude easily. Fears of judgment, not being prioritized, or abandonment keep women contained, even with their positive feelings. Even if she feels the gratitude, she doesn't show it, and that has the same effect on a man as if she didn't feel gratitude.

"May I share a problem I'm having?"

"Yes."

"I feel so grateful for you making this night special, but I feel fear of showing my joy and excitement."

"Why?"

"Because I'm afraid you'll judge me for being childish."

When a woman feels fear because of a man's potential response, she needs to tell him so he can give her reassurance, clarity, and support to fully show herself. It can take time to create that safety, but the more than she shares, and the more he responds positively, the more she can let go of her inhibitions and show the gratitude that was hiding in her heart.

The more you feel your true feelings, and express your true feelings to a man, the more that you start to heal the wounding that caused them in the first place. The more that you heal the wounding, the more room there will be to feel real gratitude. Eventually feeling it when receiving a man's gift becomes the standard. Now you need to practice expressing it using feminine communication.

When you start feeling and expressing real gratitude for a man's gifts, don't make the mistake of giving compliments. Men are not inspired into the giving role with compliments. Men with suppressed instincts might feel good receiving compliments and be compelled to covertly comply to give you more because of compliments, but it will never activate his instincts to Devote.

When my instincts were suppressed, I did enjoy compliments from women. Compliments validated my beliefs about my attractiveness because of the female attention. That was cool. But guess what? It didn't compel me into the giving role where I felt the responsibility to take care of a woman. It compelled me more into doing what a woman wanted because I enjoyed the approval. Again, the behaviors may look similar on the surface, but only one is coming from Devotion. A woman needs a man who is Devoting to her from the giving role. She doesn't need a child all bright eyed and happy because he's getting compliments from mommy for being a good boy.

Compliments don't inspire a man into the giving role because compliments are energetically masculine. When you compliment a man, you are judging him in a positive way as a gift, and he receives that gift. When a man's instincts are online, it will feel uncomfortable to receive compliments, even if they are genuine, even if they validate him in some way. I now experience this, I can't enjoy compliments from my wife because my instincts are warning me that something is 'off.' Men are the ones that are supposed to give compliments to women, women are supposed to receive compliments and feel and express gratitude for those compliments and all other gifts.

However, there is a danger of problems occurring if a woman stops giving a man compliments when she's also blocked in feeling and expressing gratitude. The compliments are like junkfood to a man. They keep him alive, but they have no nutrients to keep him healthy. Junkfood is better than nothing when you are starving to death in the wilderness. Just like compliments may be better to a man than starving from a lack of a feminine woman's gratitude. So if a woman stops complimenting her man and isn't showing gratitude in a feminine way, he may start to feel bad and get upset with her. Which keeps her stuck in a pattern of giving compliments to validate him.

The real solution though is to learn how to feel gratitude, and then learn how to express it in a feminine way.

As discussed earlier, gratitude can be as simple as a 'thankyou'. But another way to show gratitude is to use "I feel" statements.

Start with positive "I feel" statements:

"I feel happy."

"I feel excitement."

"I feel so much love in my heart right now."

"I feel awe watching you."

The 'I feel' statements will help you tap into your real feelings and express them cleanly. But understand that it's not the words that matter so much than the energy. When you were five and got all happy and excited when your dad took you for that ice-cream cone, you probably never made an 'I feel' statement. You didn't need to, because your gratitude was emanating from your voice, facial expressions, and body movement. It was obvious. That's all a man needs. He doesn't need any specific words, he just needs to feel that his gift was received.

However, the 'I feel' statements can act as fantastic training wheels to get you feeling and expressing those feelings honestly and authentically. It can get you to tap back into those feelings so that expressing gratitude can eventually be done no matter what words you use. As you practice communicating in this way, you will start feeling more deeply, and start feeling more comfortable showing your heart and all of your positive feelings. Until you learn to wear your heart on your sleeve.

Once you get to that point, it becomes far less important to make 'I feel' statements. You can if you want, but at that point you are a Jedi Master of gratitude. At this level, you couldn't hide your gratitude if you tried. It's in your smile. It's in your eyes. It's everywhere, and a man will feel it easily. He will love it, and he will give you much more love because of it.

Find that inner five year old girl inside of you, and bring her out. That is how you heal, and that is how you inspire a man to Devotionally give you the world.

CONCLUSION

WHEN YOU LEARN TO RECEIVE, YOU INSPIRE A MAN TO GIVE

My marriage has become amazing because of what I have shown you in this book. It was not an easy journey, and at times it was a very painful and frustrating journey, but the rewards have been enormous for both of us. The more that my wife learned how to receive all of my gifts, the more activated my masculine instincts became, and the more I wanted to give to her. Our relationship continues to get better to this day the more that she shifts further into the receiving role and stays there.

What I have shown you in this book is also how my clients get incredible results in their love lives. Learning how to receive gives single women the ability to effortlessly attract Devoted masculine men, and to be lovingly courted and eventually claimed as a girlfriend. Learning how to receive is also what gives partnered women the ability to inspire a man to step up, take charge, and start leading every aspect of the relationship and give them exactly what they need to thrive.

Learning to receive through your energy, communication, and behavior is the big secret for inspiring a man to give you everything you could ever need in a relationship. This secret has become obscured, inverted, and hidden because of our suppressed instincts. If every man and woman's instincts were fully online, this secret would already be known to the entire world, and everyone would be much closer to experiencing a dream relationship based on giving and receiving.

Share this secret with everyone you know who might be open to it. Tell your friends, tell your family, tell the world. Also, tell other Amazon customers about it by leaving a positive review if you loved the book. Write a paragraph about what this book has done for you or what you have learned. That's my loving directive to you, use this as an opportunity to practice receiving leadership. Not only is it good practice, but I will be grateful for your help to spread my work so that more people can transform their love lives.

You now have the power to change everything for yourself. You can make the shifts necessary to inspire a man to cherish you for the rest of your life. You can have that polarized fantasy by following what I have outlined. You deserve that kind of happiness, and it's within your reach if you choose.

But doing this will not be easy. In fact, it will almost certainly be the hardest thing you ever do. Even if you now have a general idea of what you need to do. There's a few reasons for that.

1. It's scary. Really scary. Letting go of control with a man is going against all of your learned survival patterns. It often won't feel 'safe'. If you are waiting for it to feel safe, it never will. You disempower yourself when you wait, because you are relying on someone else to help you feel comfortable being you. The level of fear, and the number of excuses you make to stay stuck in the fear will keep you stuck avoiding what you really need to do.
2. It's painful. Really painful. On this journey you will be judged by a man / men, along with other women, friends, family, and strangers. Being on the receiving end of this judgment will mean you'll likely judge yourself far more. You will sometimes be rejected. And you may be abandoned. Your needs may sometimes

not be met. Not every man will like or be inspired by you when you start shifting into the receiving role. If you're in a relationship, your man may not be instantly inspired by you shifting. When you don't get the responses you want, the pain and stories you tell yourself will compel you into giving up.

3. You will make tons of mistakes. I've outlined the basics in this book to get you started and give you a fantastic overview of how to receive a man's gifts and communicate when you are struggling to do so. But you will have your blindspots. You will misapply what I've taught. You will forget what you were supposed to do and do the wrong thing and get bad results. That's part of the learning process. Just like when you were a baby and learned how to walk, you fell down a lot. But the consequences of making mistakes with this work are far more painful than falling down on your head as a baby.
4. You won't know how to use feminine communication in every situation. There is far more depth to this work than what I have outlined here. I'd need to write a thousand books of this size to fully convey the depth and breadth of feminine communication, vulnerability, submission, and feminine self worth. There is so much more to communicating this way. While it is theoretically possible to figure it all out by trial and error like a good social scientist, the three points above are going to make that far more challenging and time consuming than it needs to be.

I do have solutions for these problems though, because I want to make this journey as easy as I can for you.

SOLUTION 1: Join our free Facebook group. With over 10,000 members, you get to be part of a huge community who are learning from my books and teachings. It's FREE.

SOLUTION 2: Read all of my other books. They all contain different pieces of the puzzle to make these shifts easier for you. The more you understand conceptually, the less mistakes you will make and the less likely you will be to give up.

SOLUTION 3: Join our 2 hour Polarized Communication Masterclass. We don't just talk about feminine communication, we demonstrate it in live roleplays. You also get to ask us questions. Seeing this in action will supercharge your understanding of what this looks like energetically and it will be a powerful belief shifting experience.

SOLUTION 4: The first three solutions are easily affordable (or in the case of the group, free). But if you know you want real expert support at helping you make these shifts, join us in my group program; the 'Relationship Of Your Dreams Academy'. This is where you will get all of the video content you need to understand what and how to shift on a far deeper level. You will get a group of hundreds of dedicated clients to ask questions, have this communication role modelled, and practice being vulnerable in a safe supportive container. You will also get one on one and group roleplay calls where we will roleplay any relevant situations to show you how to make these shifts and lovingly correct you when you misapply the teachings.

Relationship Of Your Dream Academy is focused on giving you the space to practice and refine your feminine communication and learn to receive, while we support you in your journey. We help you move through your pain, your fears, your stories, and your many inevitable mistakes. We take you on a journey from understanding this work conceptually in your head, to understanding it and shifting it in your body, fully. We facilitate your embodiment, to shift into a vulnerable feminine woman, with feminine self worth.

The Academy is more than a coaching program. It's a family. My family, that I created. For women like you.

Working with us doesn't mean we can take your fear away or make this journey painless. That would be impossible. But we can take you by the hand and make it a lot easier for you.

We can decrease the amount of time that these shifts would take. The same progress you would make in a decade or more could be made in a matter of months or up to a year. We will help you through all of your fears, and self-sabotage, and make this considerably less painful, and significantly more fun than it would be alone.

It's possible to do it all yourself. I would never lie to you and say it isn't. But you'll be paying a very heavy price in time and an unnecessary degree of painful feelings." After all, if you're a mountain climber, you could climb Mt. Everest by yourself. But with a competent team of sherpas who've got your back and show you the way with their decades of expertise, why would you attempt Mt. Everest by yourself? It would be lonely, cold and potentially deadly.

We have helped facilitate the transformations of so many men and women so that they could create the relationship of their dreams. I'd love it if you were one of the next ones.

To access any or all of the four solutions presented, go to www.relationshipofyourdreams.com

You must choose that you are worth receiving all that you want out of your love life.

And you are.

Made in the USA
Coppell, TX
15 November 2024